2 4 OCT 2012

GOS

Get **more** out of libraries

Please return or renew this item by the last date shown.
You can renew online at www.hants.gov.uk/library

Or by phoning 0845 603 5631

Hampshire
County Council

Visit our How To website at **www.howto.co.uk**

At **www.howto.co.uk** you can engage in conversation with our authors - all of whom have 'been there and done that' in their specialist fields. You can get access to special offers and additional content but most importantly you will be able to engage, and become a part of, a wide and growing community of people just like yourself.

At **www.howto.co.uk** you'll be able to talk and share tips with people who have similar interests and are facing similar challenges in their life. People who, just like you, have the desire to change their lives for the better - be it through moving to a new country, starting a new business, growing their own vegetables, or writing a novel.

At **www.howto.co.uk** you'll find the support and encouragement you need to help make your aspirations a reality.

For more information on planning your wedding and the opportunity to talk to the author Suzan St Maur visit www.planningawinterwedding.co.uk.

How To Books strives to present authentic, inspiring, practical information in their books. Now, when you buy a title from **How To Books,** you get even more than just words on a page.

Planning a
WINTER
WEDDING

SUZAN ST MAUR

howtobooks

Published by How To Books Ltd,
Spring Hill House, Spring Hill Road,
Begbroke, Oxford OX5 1RX, United Kingdom
Tel: (01865) 375794. Fax: (01865) 379162
info@howtobooks.co.uk
www.howtobooks.co.uk

How To Books greatly reduce the carbon footprint of their books
by sourcing their typesetting and printing in the UK.

British Library Cataloguing in Publication Data
A catalogue record for this book is available from the British Library

ISBN 978 1 84528 309 4

First edition 2009

Produced for How To Books by Deer Park Productions, Tavistock
Typeset by Pantek Arts Ltd, Maidstone, Kent
Printed and bound by Bell & Bain Ltd, Glasgow

Note: the material contained in this book is set out in good faith for
general guidance and no liability can be accepted for loss or expense
incurred as a result of relying in particular circumstances on statements
made in the book. Laws and regulations are complex and liable to
change, and readers should check the current position with the relevant
authorities before making personal arrangements.

Famous autumn, winter and spring weddings

HM Queen and HRH Duke of Edinburgh – 20 November 1947
HRH Prince of Wales and HRH Duchess of Cornwall – 9 April 2005
HRH Princess Royal and Captain Mark Phillips – 14 November 1973
Madonna and Guy Ritchie – 22 December 2000
Tom Cruise and Katie Holmes – 18 November 2006
Britney Spears and Kevin Federline – 6 October 2004
Paul McCartney and Linda Eastman – 12 March 1969
John Lennon and Yoko Ono – 20 March 1969
Ringo Starr and Maureen Cox – 11 February 1965
Sir Michael Caine and Shakira Baksh – 8 January 1973
Beyoncé Knowles and Jay-Z – 4 April 2008
Ivana Trump and Rossanno Rubicondi – 12 April 2008
Bill Clinton and Hillary Rodham – 11 October 1975
George Bush and Laura Welch – 5 November 1977
Président Nicolas Sarkozy and Carla Bruni – 2 February 2008
Catherine Zeta Jones and Michael Douglas – 18 November 2000
Kerry Katona and Mark Croft – 15 February 2007
Gwyneth Paltrow and Chris Martin – 5 December 2003
Colin Montgomerie and Gaynor Knowles – 19 April 2008
Elizabeth Hurley and Arun Nayar – 3 March (UK) and 9 March (India) 2007
Keith Richards and Patti Hansen – 18 December 1983
Ronnie and Jo Wood – January 1985
Marilyn Manson and Dita von Teese – 28 November 2005
Helen Mirren and Taylor Hackford – 31 December 1997
J K Rowling and Dr Neil Murray – 26 December 2001
Billie Piper and Laurence Fox – 31 December 2007
Sir Elton John and David Furnish – 21 December 2005
Michelle Heaton and Andy Scott-Lee – 20 October 2006
Phil Neville and Julie Killilea – 30 December 1999
Vic Reeves and Nancy Sorrell – 25 January 2003

Contents

Contents

Dedication

To Elizabeth, my (so far!) youngest cousin, born 2008.
Hope this book may be handy for you one day, if it's still in print.

The author

Canadian-born Suzan St Maur is a researcher, writer and author specializing in business, consumer and humour topics. She has extensive experience of writing across all media in both corporate and entertainment fields, and is also well known as a business and humorous columnist on hundreds of websites internationally. As well as writing her own material she edits other people's books, scripts and text, and advises on book preparation and publication.

Suzan has written 17 published books of her own, including the popular *Wedding Speeches For Women, The A to Z of Wedding Worries – and how to put them right*, and *How To Get Married in Green*, also by How To Books.

Suzan lives in Bedfordshire, UK, with her teenage son and various pets.

You can read more about Suzan and her work on her website: http://www.suzanstmaur.com.

Books by Suzan St Maur

- The Jewellery Book (*with Norbert Streep*) (Magnum)
- The Home Safety Book (Jill Norman Books)
- The A to Z of Video and AV Jargon (Routledge)
- Writing Words That Sell (*with John Butman*) (Management Books 2000)
- Writing Your Own Scripts and Speeches (McGraw Hill)
- The Horse Lover's Joke Book (Kenilworth Press)
- Powerwriting (Prentice Hall Business)
- Canine Capers (Kenilworth Press)
- The Food Lover's Joke Book (ItsCooking.com)
- Get Yourself Published (LeanMarketing Press)
- The MAMBA Way To Make Your Words Sell (LeanMarketing Press)
- The Easy Way To Be Brilliant At Business Writing (LeanMarketing Press)
- Wedding Speeches For Women (How To Books)

- **The Country-Lover's Joke Book** (Merlin Unwin Books)
- **The A to Z of Wedding Worries** (How To Books)
- **How To Get Married in Green** (How To Books)
- **Planning A Winter Wedding** (How To Books)

Preface

Welcome to *Planning A Winter Wedding — and how to do it in style —* and I hope you find it helpful.

I have organized the book into two parts. Part 1 is about weddings in the UK from October to April, and Part 2 goes into what's available elsewhere in the world for wedding celebrations over the same period.

Some chapters in Part 1 also include information that's relevant to Part 2 — e.g. clothes, beauty, photography — but I have cross-referenced these so you should be able to find what you're looking for.

As usual, I really have enjoyed the research process for this book and have learned a great deal, especially about opportunities for weddings around the world. I'm glad to be able to share all this with you now.

Whatever type of cooler-months wedding you choose, have a wonderful time — and many, many congratulations!

Suze

Part 1
UK-based weddings in the cooler months

Introduction

The main issue that has emerged from my research into this part of the book is that just because you choose to get married in the autumn, winter or spring in the UK does *not* necessarily mean you'll have worse weather than what you can get in the British summer.

The British climate being as unpredictable as it is means that cooler-month weddings can be just as beautiful as those at any other time. And there are distinct advantages.

Apart from peak socializing times like Christmas, New Year and Valentine's Day, wedding celebrations booked in the 'off-peak' months can be significantly cheaper than in the summertime.

Whereas in the past most people chose to get married over the summer months to ensure good weather, I believe in the last four to five years people have changed their outlook and now there is not a set time of year for a wedding season. Some venues however, do offer a sliding rate card during high and low seasons (November, January, February, March) which can be a saving of between 5% and 10% but if you are flexible on the day of the week and consider a Friday and Sunday weddings you can also benefit from different costs. But be aware of the licensing laws for a Sunday in a hotel, as they are different to the other days of the week.

Sarah Ducker
Event & Wedding Planner
www.sjdevents.com

In these cooler months, too, you have a very wide range of themes, styles, colour schemes and decorations to choose from — if anything a greater choice than you have in the summer. You're certainly not restricted to woolly clothes and roaring open fires. I hope this section of the book will set you thinking along some truly creative lines.

1 Choosing the location

Choosing the location is the first issue you need to consider, despite the fact that you may want to prioritise other things. Let's take a look at a variety of wedding locations — both in terms of the ceremony and the reception — and how the cooler months of the year might affect your choices here.

Churches and other places of worship

Naturally if you want a religious wedding ceremony in the UK you will be obliged to have it in one of the country's places of worship. Bear in mind that some of these buildings — especially some chapels and church buildings not normally cranked up for action apart from Sundays in the cooler months — are potentially draughty and damp. When planning your wedding you may want to enquire whether such a church has heating and if so, is there a charge for it to be turned on in plenty of time for your nuptials?

Nowadays the vast majority of churches, chapels and other places of worship do have heating and it will be made available for your wedding, but — especially if you're looking at a remote church or chapel in the dim and distant countryside — make sure it's available.

If you're having a religious wedding, obviously the reception will be held elsewhere, which involves the bridal party and guests needing to travel. As I've suggested below in relation to civil weddings and partnerships, such travelling between ceremony and reception can be a damp and chilly experience in the cooler months (and even in our delightful British summer, too, if you're unlucky.) In this case though, travelling is unavoidable, but to be kind to yourself and the rest of the bridal party and guests, it's probably sensible to try to arrange your reception somewhere as close as possible to the ceremony venue. Many churches have attractive church halls available for hire and these can provide a helpful solution. Although a long ramble in a vintage, open-topped car along country lanes to a charming stately pile 12 miles from the church might be a romantic prospect in flaming June, it's very unlikely to be so in November.

Having your reception at home

Unless your wedding party is going to be small, holding a reception at home is probably taking a bit of a risk. Although it's technically possible to put up and use a marquee in the cooler months (autumn and spring, certainly) the reality isn't so convenient. For starters, marquees are notoriously difficult — and expensive — to heat, and however much hot air you blow into them they still manage to be draughty and damp.

There are other little problems that can crop up too. Here's a good example: a client of mine was to give an after-dinner speech at a 'women in business' dinner, given in a marquee in November. I went along to keep her company and set up her rostrum/microphone/lighting etc. and although through the dinner we had been comfortably warm, the heat was created by giant fan heaters that looked — and sounded — like the engines from a 1960s Comet 4B jet airliner. When my client got up to speak no one could hear her even with the speakers on full blast, so we turned off the heaters. After about five minutes, the place was freezing (fabric marquees have no insulation) so my client kindly cut her speech down from 30 minutes to 15, but even then no one enjoyed it because we were all so damned cold. That taught me once and for all to advise everyone who cares to listen against using marquees in the British autumn, winter and early spring.

Civil weddings and partnerships

Here we get into a delightfully varied and abundant choice of options, despite this being what in the UK is known as the 'bad weather' time of year. This involves us taking a look at the options for civil weddings or partnerships where — ostensibly at least — you could host your reception as well.

Quite apart from other considerations like cost-savings and convenience, holding your ceremony and your reception in the same location offers yet another huge advantage in our cooler months. That's because it removes the need for you and the rest of the bridal party — plus all your guests — to bundle up, trudge through potentially wet and muddy car parks and fight your way to another venue through the rain and sleet. (I'm being particularly pessimistic here, I know!)

With ceremony and reception under one roof guests can arrive in plenty of time, check their coats in once, and then be in nice, comfortable surroundings for the whole event. And as for the bridal party, you can imagine just how much more relaxed and enjoyable the wedding will be if you don't have even to think about what the weather's doing apart from when you first arrive for the ceremony, and much later on when you depart for honeymoon or home.

Bear in mind there are, at the time of writing (mid-2008), around 4,000 venues licensed for civil weddings and partnerships in the UK and by the time you read this there may well be more. I haven't included every single category as some just aren't appropriate for cooler-month weddings (e.g. gardens with very restricted indoor space) but if you want to check out the full spread of current options, visit http://www.civilvenuesuk.com, or key '*licensed wedding venues*' into your favourite search engine.

Abbeys

There are a few of these around the country which at the time of writing are licensed to have civil weddings. Despite offering delightfully romantic surroundings in all probability they might be on the chilly side, so think carefully here.

Airports

Not only are various airports and other aviation-linked venues available as wedding venues, but also you can even get married on Concorde, based at Manchester. In your shoes, should you choose this venue, I wouldn't plan on a large reception ... Concorde was always a tight squeeze for passengers and certainly would be for a wedding venue.

Barns

There are lots of barns around the country which are licensed as civil wedding venues, if you want to have the ceremony there as well as the reception. Needless to say they have the potential to be draughty in our cooler months, but of course most have been transformed from draughty barns into highly sophisticated barn conversions.

Bingo hall

Yes, seriously. At the time of writing (mid-2008) I'm told there is a bingo hall licensed for civil ceremonies, in Hertfordshire. So if you and/or your intended are committed players and 'two little ducks,' 'two little fleas,' 'droopy drawers,' 'bull's eye', and 'snakes alive' all represent numbers to you, check it out. Could be a fascinating reception, too!

Botanical gardens, parks, etc.

At first glance your reaction to this heading might well be, 'oh, really?' but bear in mind that any garden, park etc. licensed for weddings has to do that indoors, and many of these venues actually have very attractive associated buildings which can make a lovely backdrop to a wedding even if the weather outdoors is less than friendly.

Breweries

Getting married in a brewery might be some grooms' idea of sheer Heaven, but at the time of writing it seems there is only one licensed for civil ceremonies, in north Wales. Actually, many of the older brewery premises in the UK are attractive in their own right and historically very interesting. I'm sure in time more breweries will become licensed wedding venues, and at least you won't have a problem sorting out the drinks for the reception.

Castles

Oh, this is a big one. Castles in the UK have been springing up as wedding and other function venues at an alarming rate all over the place. And where winter wedding venues are concerned, the advent of Skibo Castle — a.k.a. the Carnegie Club as I believe it's known — up in northern Scotland really did put such weddings on the map when Madonna and Guy Ritchie tied the knot there in December 2000. Similarly, recent (2008) celebrity marriages in quaint Scottish venues have included those of Ashley Judd, Ewan McGregor, and Sam Torrance.

Clubs, cricket

A few cricket clubs around the UK are licensed for weddings, including the famous Oval in London. A cricket club might not be the ideal choice unless you and/or your beloved is a keen player or fan, especially as cricket is such an 'outdoor' game and isn't played in the cold months of the year which might make the venue seem a bit bleak. For the cricket enthusiast, though, the thrill of marrying in their favourite club would be worth it all.

Clubs, football

There's a fairly wide choice of clubs licensed for weddings around country, including Chelsea, Liverpool, Man U and other famous ones. Realistically they aren't ideal if you want surroundings with romantic architecture and grand sweeping staircases à la *Gone With The Wind*, but the sheer excitement (for footie fanatics, anyway) of getting married in your very own football club would more than make up for it. Most clubs have good hospitality suites and know their way around catering, too.

Clubs, golf

Numerous golf clubs around the UK are licensed for weddings and many of them are very grand and attractive venues. They also tend to be fairly large and so are suitable for larger groups. Golf, being played all year round (my son and some friends even played in the snow once on Boxing Day using orange and pink balls), makes a good backdrop for your wedding even if you aren't a fanatic golfer yourself. Even on a chilly day as long as the light is reasonable golf courses tend to look nice outdoors for most of the year, so a few outdoor photographs will be worth a bit of a chill — provided it's not raining or snowing.

Clubs, private

A number of famous London 'gentlemen's' clubs are licensed for weddings now and you do not necessarily have to be a member to hire the venue. Many of these clubs are very attractive inside and so make a lovely backdrop for an indoor wedding; plus, they have catering facilities on site and some offer entire wedding packages including decorations, etc. They're a little on the pricey side, though, and parking in central London is a nightmare, so you would need to think of alternative transport arrangements for your guests — especially if you're having a large do.

Clubs, rugby

At the time of writing (mid-2008) there are only a few rugby clubs licensed for weddings, with the majority based in northern England. My limited experience of rugby clubs is that they tend to be smaller and more informal than football clubs, but that may just be my jaded view of beer-swilling, 7 foot, 20 stone rugby players! This would be very much a personal choice and of course if the groom is a keen player, it might be perfect. And the place will look quite lived-in, as rugby is a winter game.

Community Centres

See 'Leisure Centres' below, because most of what applies to those is relevant to Community Centres. However there might be a difference here. Community Centres tend to have contacts within their communities for things like wedding receptions and other functions, should you need to explore elsewhere for such facilities. And funnily enough, at the time of writing, a good few Community Centres around England are already licensed for civil weddings and partnerships. If you're not too fussed about baroque/Victorian/Edwardian backdrops to your wedding but just want a comfy, warm place to do the business and have a great time, this could be the right answer for you.

Country mansions

Oh, please ... in all probability there are more country mansions in the UK licensed to conduct civil marriages and partnerships than there are days in the year — no, century — so you guys have a delightful choice. Many of these places are licensed as civil wedding venues and many are also conveniently located near churches and other places of worship where a religious blessing may be carried out. In the summer months these venues often are packed out with wedding parties and although some close through the winter months, others don't. Check it all out online via your favourite search engine. In your shoes, were I sorting out a cooler-months reception in a place like this, I would be very keen to check out the heating arrangements, as often those are something the good old-fashioned Brit culture tends to forget. A ceremony in such a place is delightful, but not if everyone's fingers and toes are freezing.

Farms

Not what you'd call an obvious choice in chilly, damp weather, but many of the farms around the country licensed for weddings are in fact conversions from farms to proper function suites with all the trimmings. So you don't have to get married in a barn and have your photographs done while standing in pigswill! My own feeling is that a farm location could be a bit dreary in mid-winter, but the autumn or spring might well be good times. Some are fairly small, so are only suitable for smaller groups.

Hotels

It will come as no surprise to you that, at the time of writing, there are hundreds of hotels licensed for civil weddings and partnerships in the UK and by the time you read this book it's likely there will be dozens, scores, or hundreds more. Not that this is a bad thing; hotels often offer a far more attractive setting for your ceremony than the local Registry Office and not only can you reduce the carbon footprint of your wedding by having your reception in the same place, but also you can save your guests having to put their coats on and traipse/drive to a reception somewhere else, even before and after your wedding, should they happen to book into rooms there. The potential downside of hotels in the cooler months of the year is that – perhaps because they are so convenient for such things – they do tend to get booked up well in advance. The pre-Christmas weeks are a particularly bad time to think hotels with 'banqueting' facilities because they will be given over to business Christmas parties. However, during the months of October,

The main advantage is that couples can pretty much have the pick of venues and as it is a quieter time of year they usually offer great discounts for weddings. Hotels will also wish to fill rooms and may offer reduced rates for block bookings. Make sure you ask for out-of-season rates when viewing venues.

Emma Glen
Behind the Veil Wedding Planning Service
www.behindtheveil.co.uk

9

November, January (after New Year), February and March, many hotels are quiet on the function side and can be persuaded to supply a wedding package that's pretty good value for money.

Leisure Centres

At the time of writing, there are a few leisure centres around the UK licensed for weddings and I imagine — and hope — that this number will grow. Although leisure centres tend to be modern establishments geared to sports and fitness stuff and therefore are not necessarily designed to be pretty and picturesque, many of them do offer some very good value for private functions (I used places like this for my son's birthday parties when he was little) and increasingly they are offering more interesting packages — especially 'out of season,' i.e. in autumn, winter and spring months. Their prices seem to be very reasonable and if you want to have a large crowd at your wedding, they usually can provide a lot of space, albeit not necessarily with much style or panache.

Mills

Although these licensed wedding venues — of which currently there is only a handful in England — originally will have functioned as working mills, all that will tend to have been a long time ago and in the meantime they will have morphed into modern conference, banqueting and other function sites. Bear in mind that not all mills were particularly picturesque indoors, and that may still be the case, with the venues relying more on the attractiveness of their grounds. Not necessarily the best choice in our cooler months.

Mines and caverns

Yes, really. There are a few in the English West Country and Wales licensed for civil weddings and partnerships. Well, such a wedding would surely be different, but remember to tell your photographer to bring plenty of lighting. Also, good luck with getting the catering in there, and keep your guest list pretty short.

Museums

There are numerous museums around the country licensed for wedding ceremonies and they can provide a backdrop for your wedding that has great character and panache. I suspect they offer good photo opportunities, too; the weather may not be kind enough to permit photographs being taken in the grounds, but a group shot clustered around a dinosaur skeleton or vintage car is quite a reasonable alternative. Museums, being used principally in the warmer months, may not have quite such efficient heating systems as you would want in frosty January, and you're likely to have to bring in all catering.

Night clubs

Amazingly, at the time of writing, it appears there is only one night club licensed for weddings — in the north-west of England. To me it's a shame there aren't more, if only because night clubs are ideally suited to weddings when the weather outside isn't so good, with appropriate seating, dramatic lighting and in-built sound systems for dancing. With luck more such venues will come on stream before long.

Orangeries

Crudely speaking an orangery is a cross between a sunny room and a conservatory. There are a few licensed as wedding venues around the country and they make good wedding venues in the darker months of the year because, with a lot of windows and glass in the ceilings, etc., they provide as much natural light as you're going to get anywhere. That can be quite helpful for your wedding photographs provided you time them appropriately, and orangeries tend to be pretty places anyway so lending themselves to a romantic event. If this is your choice, make sure the heating works well.

Pavilions and piers

I suppose it's not surprising that, at the time of writing, there are few pavilions and piers around the UK up for grabs as civil ceremony venues, if only because the vast majority are located in places where good weather in the cooler months is extremely unlikely and overall facilities are — shall we say — potentially difficult to implement. Brighton Pier, however, is not one of them so we're told and can provide most of the facilities you'd need for a reception as well as a ceremony venue. How you get there from the shore should the weather be unkind I'm not sure, not without getting pretty cold, wind-swept and wet anyway, but the option is there nonetheless. And in the autumn and spring months, the UK climate (in the south at least) can be kind enough to make such a wedding a delightful venue — even for those outdoor photographs.

Pubs, inns and wine bars

As you would expect there are numerous pubs and inns around the country licensed as wedding venues, but incredibly (at the time of writing) there's only one wine bar — in the north-west of England. When we talk about pubs and inns here we're looking at traditional types of venue rather than places from the 'nouveau' wave of gastro pubs and American-styled pseudo inns. These are mainly older establishments with low ceilings, narrow doorways, dim lighting and lots of genuine character. Not normally appropriate for larger weddings, but cosy and delightful for a smaller winter wedding with lots of charm and goodwill.

Racecourses

A fair few racecourses around the country are licensed for weddings and if your wedding date should coincide with their racing seasons, you could even combine your nuptials with a flutter on the gee-gees. (Some racing goes on throughout most of the year.) As indoor venues, racecourses are likely to be efficient in catering terms but not necessarily all that picturesque, and in the chilly, damp months the exteriors can be muddy and miserable. If this is your choice, some creative indoor photography will be required.

Railway stations

At the time of writing, there is a handful of historic railway stations up for grabs as licensed wedding venues and should you and/or your beloved be a train buff, this could be the choice for you. Bear in mind though, that such places may not have very sophisticated heating systems and might even close during our cooler months. Also, because the buildings tend to be compact, they may not be suitable for anything other than a small group. Plus of course, you'll need to bring in catering etc., should you decide to hold your reception there as well.

Restaurants

Just as in the case of pubs and inns, numerous restaurants around the UK have acquired licenses for wedding in recent times and when you consider our purposes here — i.e. weddings and receptions in the cooler, damper months — you could be excused for thinking a restaurant is probably an ideal venue.

Restaurants do tend to offer a year-round environment and atmosphere and those combine to make some of them, at least, good news places to host a wedding, particularly a small one. For a large wedding party, the choice of restaurants is likely to be relatively small, although some restaurants have private suites that can cope with quite a few people.

Schools, private

Many of our older, traditional 'public' schools have had to up their income despite huge fees being paid by parents, and offering themselves as licensed wedding venues is one way to add to the coffers. A number of these schools – mostly in southern England – do this and because so many of them are in beautiful historic premises, they're really quite appealing. Whether on-site catering would be appropriate is another matter; if this is your choice you might like to consider bringing in your own caterers for the reception unless you especially want bangers and mash and toad-in-the-hole! Ah, seriously, these places can be a good choice and because their interiors can be very attractive, may be especially suitable for interior photography. They also tend to be large and so suitable for larger crowds. You may find you can only book during school holidays, which would be the half term weeks late October/early November and late February, plus Christmas and Easter holidays (which tend to be longer than those of state schools).

Special venues

Here I've touched on a few venues in the UK which are unique and really don't fall into any other category other than their own. By the time you read this, there could well be many more. So watch that space on your favourite search engine.

- But for now, for starters, we have **Blackpool Tower**. Now, realistically the weather in the north-west of England isn't always too clever in our cooler months but you can get lucky, and think what a wedding out of season in Blackpool could return in cost-saving terms, as well as all the fun? Naturally, the Tower is licensed for civil weddings and its ballroom can be, quite simply, a stunning indoor venue capable of hosting quite a large group.

- Next is **Brighton** on England's south coast, which offers a number of interesting and unusual licensed wedding venues like the **Brighton Sea Centre** (I've been there — it's modern, amazing, and all indoors) ... **Brighton Pavilion** ... something of a folly created by a Prince of Wales and now a treasured — and beautifully conserved — piece of English history ... **Brighton Pier** (have also been there, many, many times when my son was little — he loved it and of course most of it is under cover) ... and **Brighton Racecourse**, which is delightful but tends only to operate in early autumn or late spring.

- The **London Eye** — yes, you can get married on that great big cartwheel by the bank of the River Thames, at a height of 135 metres above London, to be precise. Bearing in mind that the individual capsules do not take all that many travellers, you'd probably be wise to avoid inviting more than a small number of guests. But a variety of civil wedding and partnership packages are available if this is what you'd like to do ... snacks, champagne and all.

- **Tower Bridge** is another location licensed for weddings and capable of hosting receptions ... and what a piece of English history! It probably isn't suitable for large gatherings but for smaller groups, it's worth considering. The weather may be cold and wet outside, but at least the Thames is consistently interesting year-round.

- **Ships and submarines** ... yes, there are a good few ships tied up along UK docks which are licensed for civil weddings and partnerships and some of them are really sublime as venues not only for the ceremony but also your reception, too. Obviously they offer shelter from the elements and, we hope, heating sufficient to keep you, your bridal party and all your guests as warm as toast. Catering is available in most cases, but you would be well advised to check it out carefully and if you're not happy, contemplate bringing in your own.

- **Windmill** ... There is one windmill in England that's licensed for civil weddings and partnerships — it's in Norfolk, and at the time of writing, they are booked up for quite some months ahead whether in peak season or not. Only suitable for relatively small groups.

Sports stadiums

For sports and athletics enthusiasts there are a number of sports stadiums licensed in the UK and as most have reasonable-sized hospitality suites can make a good cooler-months venue if they are under cover. Whether the absence of athletes competing and a cheering crowd might make such a place a little empty for your nuptials is not for me to say; certainly if you and/or your spouse-to-be is a keen athlete the romance of marrying within such a location would overcome any emptiness.

Studios, film and TV

A very few film and TV studios are licensed for marriages, mostly in the south-east of England. Having worked there quite a lot at one time in my career, I can vouch for Pinewood being a lovely venue, although much of its olde-worlde charm is connected with the exterior; the interior is rather more business-like these days. All the same, if you're a film or TV buff, the thought of tying the knot where Bond films and other famous epics are made, will be sheer magic.

Theatres and cinemas

Although at the time of writing there are only a few cinemas licensed for weddings in the UK — mostly in the south-east — there are numerous theatres so licensed, including some of the most famous ones in the West End of London. Although hiring such a theatre is not likely to be cheap, it will provide a very romantic and charismatic backdrop to your wedding, especially if you and yours are thespians and/or theatre buffs. Being in a city centre these theatres do not depend much on being picturesque on the exterior, but their interiors can be absolutely breath-taking.

Theme parks

At the time of writing, there is only one theme park licensed for weddings, in Gloucestershire. By the time you read this there may be more, but bear in mind that theme parks in the UK tend to close down from the autumn half-term week in the UK until the Easter break, so are unlikely to find opening up for weddings and other such functions a viable business proposition. Even if they did, they would probably be something of a dreary location in the colder months and the absence of laughing children, music, ice cream, candy floss, hair-raising rides and warm weather do not (in my humble opinion) add up to an inspiring wedding venue. However, watch this space; theme parks of the future may focus more on indoor pursuits in which case they could become much more appealing.

Universities

Universities offer options similar to those of schools, although some of the 'redbrick' colleges are even more attractive inside and out and can provide a superb backdrop for your wedding even if it the gales are howling outdoors. As with schools you may find you can only book here during the vacations, but those of universities tend to be longer than those of schools so you should get a reasonable choice of dates in December/January and then also around two weeks either side of Easter.

Vineyards

As I write this a small handful of vineyards venues are licensed for civil weddings and partnerships in the UK – mainly in the south of England. However, as wine production continues to grow in the UK – in, part, we're assured, due to global warming and all that – vineyard weddings show every sign of burgeoning accordingly. It's not unreasonable to suppose that further wine-growing venues will become available and of course, particularly in the autumn months, a wedding held at a vineyard is going to be not only seasonal, but also it will be a great opportunity for wine buffs to enjoy themselves.

Zoos

London Zoo, in particular, claims to offer ideal surroundings and circumstances for Jewish and Asian Weddings as well as the civil variety. Certainly they are well set up for a good party. There are a few other zoos around the country offering wedding services, too.

Small wedding locations

If you're looking at a very small wedding, this could be the time of year when a ceremony and celebrations abroad could end up giving you (a) a wonderful time and (b) some very good value. For a choice of locations and what they offer in our cooler months, see Part Two.

If on the other hand you decide to stay in the UK, there are lots of options that are not weather dependent and yet can provide a superb backdrop for a wedding to treasure forever. Here are a few ideas to set you thinking.

Restaurants

These are excellent places to hold small wedding celebrations and now that numerous restaurants around the country are licensed for civil ceremonies as well, with the appropriate choice you can combine the two elements and probably obtain an excellent deal. Provided that you avoid the obvious peak times like the run-up to Christmas and New Year, Valentine's Day and Easter, many restaurants tend to be a bit on the quiet side — especially at the week-end when their business trade may drop off. Depending on the size of the restaurant and the size of your group, they may not even need to close the place to other business, so giving you the opportunity to drive an even harder bargain.

Clubs

Clubs — especially but not exclusively golf clubs — can offer some attractive propositions for small wedding groups and as many are now licensed for civil ceremonies may well have all the facilities you need under one roof. If you or a close relative is a member of such a club, you may be able to negotiate a particularly good deal, especially during the months when only the 19th hole is well attended whatever the weather. It's usually easy to find out what bookings a club has over the autumn, winter and spring months well in advance, and unlike hotels and restaurants a club is unlikely to be over-run with external bookings throughout the holiday seasons. Another benefits of clubs — golf clubs in particular — is that they usually offer a lot of parking space. And, if you're lucky with the weather, a few wedding pix shot by the putting green, the driving range or the first tee can add to your fond memories, especially if you are keen golfers.

Private clubs

Private clubs, e.g. some of the more famous 'gentlemen's clubs' in London, offer a quirky but nostalgic environment for a small wedding and in most cases, some lovely interior backdrops for your photographs. Whether you need a membership connection or not depends on the club in question. If it's a London club (and the vast majority of those licensed for civil weddings are, although of course you can just have your reception in a club after a religious or civil wedding elsewhere) you'll find parking a bit of a problem, but then that's something anyone dealing with London has to navigate! In fact parking in central London on weekends, especially late on Saturdays and on Sundays, is not so difficult and as you're having a small group you don't need spaces for 100 cars.

Hotels

Hotels are an obvious choice whether you want a ceremony and reception venue all in one, or the hotel purely for your reception. That's largely because (a) hundreds of UK hotels are licensed for civil ceremonies and (b) many hotels have this amazing capacity to morph from tiny function rooms to function rooms that accommodate hundreds, within hours, although in fairness these tend to be the ultra-modern, ultra-tech places that you may wish to avoid, especially if you're going to be a small group. With a small group, you're ideally placed to opt for a smaller, older hotel that potentially offers a lot of character, ambience and romance — such a great backdrop for the whole event, not merely the photographs. And the bonus is that you, your bridal party and possibly all your guests, too, can book rooms in the place and not have to worry about anything other than crawling up to bed after a wonderful party.

Pubs

These are another option for a small wedding group, and as there are quite a few now licensed as civil wedding venues this is a reasonable consideration, particularly if the pub in question is one with which you have emotional or social ties. The downside of pubs is that they tend to have either no or else limited overnight accommodation facilities, and varying availability of car parking spaces. However, what they do offer that many other types of venue do not, is character — and lots of it. Just the right environment for an informal, cosy and joyful small wedding party and provided there are plenty of old beams, inglenook fireplaces, collections of brass ornaments and antique-style furniture, a wonderful backdrop for your photographs.

Country houses

Country houses are also up for grabs for both ceremonies and receptions and are likely to be a lot more open to downwards negotiation on price during our cooler months if, indeed, they are open at all. With so many now licensed for civil ceremonies and linked up with suppliers to provide catering and all other requirements, you may like to consider this one seriously for a 'cooler months' backdrop. Even if it's raining outside the Georgian façade you're still likely to find some gorgeous surroundings for your pictures indoors.

Other appropriate venues

These are wide and varied and can be found if you key **'small weddings'+venues** into your favourite search engine. At the time of writing, there are quite a few potential candidates here but none more entertaining — and potentially breathtaking — than getting married in a pod on the London Eye. Yes, such a thing is licensed as a civil ceremony venue despite being as much as 135 metres above the deck and your capsule will be decorated not only with flowers but a good few snifters of excellent champagne. You'll need to seek a further reception venue elsewhere though, once you come down to earth ... go to http://www.londoneye.com for more information.

2 Deciding on hen and stag celebrations

In traditional circles, people often feel that a pre-nuptial hen or stag celebration — particularly the stag variety — needs to involve a great deal of hilarity, drunkenness, outrageous behaviour and severe hangovers if it is to be remembered as an event of note.

Now, I'm in no position to criticize that notion, especially when you consider what we girls got up to on my hen night, but that's not relevant here! Frankly, if this is the kind of hen or stag celebration that appeals to you, quite honestly, you can do that almost anywhere — indoors or out.

However, there can be more to a hen or stag celebration, especially as they provide a useful opportunity for friends and family members of all ages to bond and get to know each other prior to the wedding. Increasingly these days, couples are choosing less alcoholic options, or at least those combined with non-alcoholic activities, to make their pre-nup party extra special.

Going abroad

During the UK cooler months, you can get some excellent deals in many European and North American locations, as this is the low season for them and they tend, understandably, to be keen to promote their wares for hen/stag celebrations.

European (and North American) capital cities are an obvious target for hen and stag celebrations, particularly if you and your party are not too fussy about the weather outdoors. You can find out more about individual locations in Part 2, but suffice it to say here that a great time 'can be had by all' at prices that can be very attractive, especially if you're willing to savour cities in our relatively new EC member countries. Key '***city breaks***' into your favourite search engine.

Mediterranean resorts have a way of offering unbelievably good deals in our cooler months, but be warned. In all but the very large or fashionable resorts many restaurants, bars, clubs and even hotels are likely to be closed during the cold months. Weather at this time can, of course, be lovely — but equally it can be rainy and a bit on the chilly side.

So if you're attracted by a very cheap deal on a Balearic Island, for example, remember that those iconic clubs that throb through the night in the summer could well be boarded up now, and your party could be restricted to karaoke evenings in the largest hotel on the island. And if it's raining? It may well not matter, especially if your interests lie largely within an indoor environment. But for any outdoor activity — especially swimming — it really isn't safe to count on sunny Spain/Portugal/south of France/south of Italy/Greece either after about December, or before March.

Locations in the southern hemisphere are unlikely to produce any great bargains as these months represent their medium to high seasons. However, if you want to spend the money, the weather in these places can be at its best.

Needless to say the hen and stag celebration market has attracted the attention of numerous businesses and if you key '***hen celebration***' or '***stag celebration***' into your favourite search engine you'll find quite a few specialist organizations you can contact for ideas, arrangements and bookings. Do be careful to choose an established, respected company, though. Recently I've heard a number of accounts of hen and particularly stag groups lured to a romantic city or resort via very cheap flights and accommodation, only to find that on arrival they are escorted to a series of bars and clubs where the organizers rack their profits back up again by charging ludicrous prices for entry and drinks. They assume that party members will be drunk most of the time and won't realise how much they've spent until after they get home and read their credit card statements.

How about here in the UK?

If you want to stay at home in the UK, let's have a look at some cold/wet weather options that can combine the traditional liquid indoor celebrations if you want, but add a certain extra something. Deliberately I have not differentiated between activities suited more — in my personal view — to women than men, because (a) my views are entirely irrelevant and (b) these days anything goes, especially considering that we're talking both traditional weddings and civil partnerships here.

Archery

There are many options for archery days and weekends in the UK. These are mostly outdoors, but in theory the sport is a year-round one and provided that it's not raining or snowing this might be fun. Probably best considered for autumn and spring months, not mid-winter. Key '**archery packages**' into your favourite UK search engine for current offerings.

Beer tasting

This seems to be a relatively new concept here in the UK; at the time of writing (mid-2008) there are only six listings for private beer tasting on Google. However by the time you read this that number is likely to have grown. For a hen or stag do (dare I say that maybe it might be more appreciated by the guys? Or is that because I am definitely *not* a beer drinker?) this one is worth looking into. Key '**private beer tasting**' into your favourite search engine.

City breaks

In our haste to experience foreign scenery and cheaper booze in continental European cities, we often forget what beautiful and fascinating cities there are to enjoy here in the UK. Various packages are available to pretty well all our more interesting cities and prices in the off-season months can be very reasonable indeed. Even if the weather is bad, there will still be plenty to do in terms of shopping, sight-seeing, indoor locations like museums, cinemas and theatres, plus a host of new restaurants, pubs and clubs. Check out '**UK city breaks**' on your favourite search engine.

Clay pigeon shooting

Clay pigeon shooting grounds are out of doors, of course, but unless it is bitterly cold and wet shooting clays is good fun, and also is an activity which can be enjoyed by everyone regardless of age, gender or ability unless severely disabled. Once again, autumn and spring would be preferable times to choose this, rather than mid-winter. More information is available from http://www.cpsa.co.uk.

Cocktail making class

This is a good one if you want to learn something and get tiddly at the same time. At the time of writing (mid-2008) there are a good few businesses offering private cocktail making classes and demonstrations, some specifically geared for hen and stag celebrations. Currently these tend to happen only in the larger cities like Edinburgh, Manchester, London, etc. Also I have heard of a couple of companies offering to run such a class in your home, or in the venue of your choice; key '***private cocktail making class***' into your favourite search engine.

Comedy clubs

These, not surprisingly, are very popular venues for hen and stag nights and provide not only the party atmosphere and booze required, but also some hilarious entertainment. The bad news is that they tend only to exist in our larger cities, so if you and your group are not based close by, this makes it more difficult — although of course you could combine an evening in a comedy club with a UK city break. Key '***comedy clubs***' into your favourite search engine.

Dancing

This is a very popular activity and various classes have sprung up almost everywhere in the last few years for such dance genres as salsa, jive, flamenco, line, latin, belly, ballroom and many more. You can even get private tuition in 'dirty' or pole dancing — a nifty idea for a hen night, the outcome of which could make for some interesting dancing at your wedding reception! Key '***dance lessons***' into your favourite search engine.

Driving, off road

Ironically, you could say that the worse the weather, the more fun offroading can be; there's nothing like pouring rain and deep mud to enhance the experience of driving a 4x4/SUV up and down slithering hillsides. Not necessarily a good idea for the girlies, although many girlies are very good at offroad driving, but it certainly will keep the boys on their toes. Key '**offroad driving**' into your favourite search engine.

Driving, racing

A number of organizations offer racing driving experience events and these do take place almost all year round, although once again mid-winter is probably best avoided. Unless there is heavy rain or the temperature is well below freezing, you'll enjoy a drive around a racetrack in a sports or single seater car. In fact if anything this is more enjoyable in cooler weather, as even UK summer temperatures can be quite uncomfortable when you're out there. Key '**race driving**' into your favourite search engine.

Fencing

A challenging sport but one — the basics of which — you can learn on a relatively quick basis. Needless to say it's perfectly safe and the only thing likely to receive a dent is your ego. The sport is quite tightly regulated in the UK so if you wanted to arrange a fencing tuition weekend, say, you would probably need to do it in association with one of the many fencing clubs in the UK. Contact http://www.britishfencing.com.

Football and rugby

Assuming you and the rest of your party all support the same football or rugby team, an obvious choice of weekend away is a trip to watch your team play. Bear in mind, though, that you may not want your stag (or hen) celebrations to be eclipsed by the agonies or ecstasies of your team's score and new place in the league.

Go-karting

This is great fun, you don't have to be 17 or have a driving licence to do it, and nowadays there are numerous indoor venues which means the sport is not weather-dependent. Some of these venues have catering facilities and will organize a party for you, but it's very unlikely that they will allow any alcohol to be consumed anywhere near the karts or driving time. It's a terrific way to spend a morning or afternoon of your hen or stag UK weekend though.

Health spa

This is a very popular choice for hen celebrations all year round, but especially in the cooler months as you can spend anything up to a week in one of these places and not venture outdoors at all. Apart from enjoying all the treatments and pampering, you can usually enjoy excellent (healthy) food in their restaurants and although you might get the odd disapproving look, you should also be able to order wine with your meals and have drinks elsewhere, too.

Jewellery making

In the UK there are numerous opportunities for jewellery making courses offered by a wide variety of companies and individuals. Not only would such an activity be interesting as a hen celebration but also might result in some stunning contributions to the wedding picture, both for the key participants and for everyone else! Key '*jewellery making*' into your favourite search engine.

Makeover

This can be a good laugh at worst and at best, an incredible opportunity to review your look and wardrobe for the next ten years. At the time of writing, there are a few companies offering makeover sessions and weekends in the UK, and by the time you read this it's likely there will be more. Not one the boys will gravitate towards, necessarily, but an interesting exercise for anyone. Key '*makeover weekends*' into your favourite search engine.

Medieval evening

Numerous venues and locations offer medieval nights, weekends and other celebrations, many of which take place under cover — even medieval banquets with an accompanying cabaret of jousting on horseback. It is an unusual and interesting way to spend a stag or hen evening. Key '*medieval parties*' into your favourite search engine.

Murder weekend

Not exactly a new idea but a great favourite, especially in the winter months. Also they are ideal for a group of mixed ages, interests and physical abilities. As you know, these involve actors playing out a 'grisly' murder setup in the venue concerned and you and your group must be the detectives and solve the crime. All good clean fun, especially accompanied by delicious food and booze. Some companies offer murder evenings as well as weekends, and some will also organise an event for you at a venue of your choice.

Paintballing

Although you wouldn't want to go around a paintballing course in deep snow, heavy rain or thick frost, in the autumn and spring months this is a distinct possibility and as you're likely to get muddy and dirty whatever the weather, you may as well enjoy it outside of our summer months. There are numerous paintballing organizations around the country so you shouldn't have any trouble finding one near you, and in the cooler — i.e. off-season — months you may well be able to negotiate a very good deal.

Pottery making

This is a popular activity for children's parties but adult versions do exist and are equally popular — there's nothing like rolling up your sleeves and digging your hands into that clay. And this could be an ideal opportunity to make some bespoke favours for the wedding reception. Just make sure you leave time for a good manicure before the wedding day. Several UK companies offer inclusive courses, weekends, days, etc. Key '**pottery parties**' into your favourite search engine.

Quad biking

If you and your group are the outdoor types and fancy this kind of challenge, you'll find it's still a distinct possibility in the autumn and spring months — especially as muddy fields and chilly cross country courses are all part of the fun. Not an activity I would choose in mid-winter, but then I'm old and boring.

Tank driving

Okay, this is a bit of a hairy-chested option but weather — or cold — really don't affect the thrill you'll get from piloting a huge machine over rough terrain and getting in touch with your more rugged self. Numerous organizations offer this activity for a variety of purposes including pre-wedding celebrations — just key '**tank driving**' into your favourite search engine.

Tennis, badminton, squash, etc

If you and your hen or stag party all play one of these games and you have a facility locally where you can do these things indoors, you could organise a tournament. Many clubs offering such facilities also offer bars, restaurants and even private catering facilities so you could arrange an entire hen or stag celebration here.

Thai massage

There are numerous individuals and organizations around who both teach and practice this delightful stuff and whether you want to indulge your bridal party in receiving it, learning it, or both, this could be a very suitable activity for a hen celebration during our cooler months. As it happens a great friend of mine, Ana Benedict, is an expert in this field so if you want more information on that topic you should email ana@stressresponse.com She'll advise you on opportunities in your area.

Wine tasting

Numerous companies offer bespoke wine tasting sessions for a variety of different private functions of which hen and stag celebrations form a significant part. This can be done locally, via a local or regional wine merchants, or if you key '**private wine tasting**' into your favourite search engine you'll find people who will bring such a session to the venue of your choice, to your own specifications. Once again this has the obvious advantage of combining a cultural activity with having a few drinks, although ostensibly proper wine tasting should involve you spitting out the various samples to prevent your palate from being damaged by a little bit of drunkenness.

3 Choosing themes

Of course you may not want to theme your wedding to the season concerned, particularly if it's happening at a relatively dull time of the year. However, don't be put off by the fact that the daylight hours are short and the weather is chilly and damp. As it happens, there are many excuses to celebrate in the autumn, winter and spring months in the UK and elsewhere – and a resultant number of lovely ideas that you can weave into your wedding.

General autumn themes

Although here in the UK and northern Europe we aren't normally blessed by quite such a riot of colour and abundance as you'll find in, say, north America, we still do have some lovely things to enhance our lives and some glorious themes to use for decorations and more.

You can incorporate the gentle auburns, golds, chartreuses and chestnut shades of the turning leaves into a stunning colour combination.

If you want to look further towards vegetation for inspiration, think about apples ... pears ... grapes ready for harvesting and wine production ... not to mention the wide variety of autumn flowering plants, like chrysanthemums to name but one ... all of which can be incorporated into your wedding theme and beyond (e.g., as wedding favours, bases for menu options, etc.)

Should you want to enjoy a particularly informal theme, look to the farms and the recent harvests ... hay and straw bales as well as traditional autumn items like corn dollies and harvest baskets provide lovely, rustic decorative opportunities as well as opportunities to provide guests with take-home favours that (a) reflect the theme of your wedding and (b) are eco-friendly.

Getting on towards late October you can also consider pumpkins and their related species as decorative ideas, even if you'd prefer not to go the whole hog with a Halloween theme. If you can find small pumpkins in the UK (you may need to work with someone who has a large vegetable garden or allotment here) you can hollow them out as use them as vases on tables, filled with autumn flowers and greenery – a beautiful acknowledgement of the season.

Moving even further on through the autumn months, don't forget the lovely 'conkers' – chestnuts which can echo through your wedding theme with their vibrant, ruby-brown colour and delicious taste when roasted and/or incorporated into your wedding menu.

And don't forget the artistic opportunities afforded by the autumn leaves and other foliage, even for such things as representative decorations on invitations, place cards and other printed material as well as within floral and other actual displays. Their richness and depth of colour really will create some vibrant effects.

We often use fruits and vegetables in the Autumn which create a wonderful textured feel to the designs. Flowers in the autumn are typically quite textured (a lot available are almost spiky in appearance). Then we get into winter and brides can choose to go for a more traditional feel with reds and greens with typically winter flowers and foliages or they can go down the winter wonderland style of lots of twigs and fairy lights with candelabras etc.

I would advise my brides marrying during these months to try and use seasonal flowers whenever possible and try to include the 'feel' of the season into their design. I have designed pink weddings in autumn by using very seasonal materials we can still create the autumnal feel with a summery colour – for instance in one wedding we used pomegranates cut in half which gave us the bright red/cerise colour which worked beautifully with a pink theme and gave an autumnal feel to the arrangements.

Beverley Nichols
Jades Flower Design
http://www.jadesflowers.co.uk

Specific autumn themes

As I suggested above, unlike — in some ways — the summer months, the autumn, winter and spring months provide quite a wide choice of events around which you might like to theme your wedding. Let's now take a look at some of them. Given the scope of this book (and my limit of the number of words I could write!), I have mentioned as many as possible. However, bear in mind that this list is far from conclusive and especially if you come from a culture other than those of western Europe or North America, there are many, many more options. So here are my few.

Canadian Thanksgiving — early October

Needless to say, Canadian Thanksgiving is very similar to the American version, except that the occasions occur at different times: the Canadian version takes place on the second Monday of October (thereby creating a 'long weekend'). It's generally thought that the reason why the Canadian Thanksgiving takes place several weeks earlier than the American version is because the Canadian harvest, being obviously further north, takes place earlier in general terms than it does in the USA.

What is really lovely about Thanksgiving in North America (whether in Canada or the USA) is that it is a major family gathering of the year — in some ways, particularly in the USA, almost more important than Christmas — and affords opportunities for some lovely decorative and gastronomic enjoyment.

Key here are the vibrant colours of autumn and the close, cosy atmosphere created when family and close friends gather together to stop and think about their good fortune to be alive and thriving. What better theme for a wedding!

Apart from choosing autumn colours and other allied physical decorations, you may like to include the thoughts of Thanksgiving into your wedding vows and carry those on out into your communications, vows, and even speeches. Whatever religion you may follow, we in industrialized countries have a lot to be thankful for and to incorporate such sentiments into a wedding can help to make it especially memorable.

Halloween – 31 October

And now, for something completely different! Elderly relatives and other wedding guests who treasure traditional views would be horrified at the thought of a Halloween themed wedding, but believe me people do use this for wedding themes (and even more bizarre ideas) ... so if this takes your fancy, don't be shy.

I suppose where people could argue that Halloween is a bad idea to connect with a wedding is because of all the ancient superstitions attached to it. Let's face it, they are hardly appropriate. But provided that you don't take all that too seriously and just enjoy the fun of the occasion, a Halloween themed wedding could be great fun, especially if your wedding is to be small, informal and appeal to your younger guests. Children will love this theme and everyone can join in the fun with costumes, games, etc.

You need to think in terms of colours based on orange and black, the traditional Halloween hues. Within that you can also incorporate all shades of orange through to yellow and white, plus some sparkling and glittery items in silvers and golds.

If you want to take decorations to the limit, consider cobwebs, fake bats, spiders and other insects and of course, skeletons. Needless to say you'll want the reception area dimly lit, preferably with candles, accompanied by Jack O Lanterns by the dozen – made from hollowed out pumpkins with tealights or short candles inserted therein.

A small tip here, which comes from personal experience. If you use Jack O Lanterns made from real pumpkins, although you may be advised to replace the 'lids' (which you've cut out in order to hollow the pumpkins out) ... don't. That's for the simple reason that with lids on, and candles inside, the lanterns will soon begin to cook the underside of the lids and create a slightly inappropriate smell ... not to mention the demise of the lantern rather earlier than you would like. Lidless, however, the lanterns can keep going for some hours.

Bonfire Night – 5 November

The Americans celebrate Independence Day with fireworks on 4 July, the French celebrate with fireworks on Bastille Day which is 14 July, and in the UK? We let our fireworks off at the end of autumn when the weather is unlikely to be help-ful, but so what? Here's an excuse for a glorious wedding theme.

Unless you really want to get historical and relive the Gunpowder Plot *in extremis*, probably all you need to consider here is the fact that fireworks are called for. Obviously if you want to take the theme more seriously you will choose a relaxed, casual approach involving a reception that focuses on an outdoor bonfire, simple outdoor-based food (see Chapter 6) and the lovely warmth and comfort of a totally informal, fun-based wedding reception.

Still taking the theme seriously, you may also decide to let the fireworks off earlier rather than later, so that the kids can enjoy them too. (So many wed-dings include firework displays at midnight or later, which rather cheats the little ones out of their fun.)

As far as clothing, décor and other accessories are concerned, you may want to go the whole hog and go for an early 17th century look throughout. Good luck if you do! For further inspiration here key '*gunpowder plot*' into your favourite search engine.

However a 21st century Bonfire Night wedding can mainly take into account the bonfire, fireworks, casual conditions and casual food and drink we in the UK have come to associate with this occasion. This theme works best for a small, informal wedding group and preferably with the reception being held at a private home with room in the garden for the bonfire and fireworks. Some commercial venues may be prepared to let you have a bonfire and certainly fireworks on their premises, but this may fall foul of health and safety regula-tions and not be included in the venue's insurance policy.

Diwali – October or November

Interestingly enough many people say that Diwali has its roots as a harvest festival, not unlike its western equivalents in Europe and North America.

Diwali is celebrated not merely in India, where it originates, but in numerous countries around the world. And whether you celebrate Diwali for religious rea-sons or not, it provides a wonderful theme for a colourful, bright wedding at a time of year when our northern European skies are usually at their darkest.

Things that exemplify Diwali are bright, colourful clothes and jewellery (and perhaps an Indian themed wedding dress — see Chapter 4) as well as fire-works and endless sparklers, radiating paper lanterns and other decorations, plus sweet treats and gifts all round.

But above and beyond that is the strong focus on light. Whether it's provided by endless candles and tealights, oil lamps (in the traditional way) or groups of lamps blended together as decorative features, electric equivalents both indoors and out and even gigantic lighting creations that illuminate a whole neighbourhood, Diwali can inspires some wonderful wedding ideas.

There are many useful websites to give you more ideas about a Diwali themed wedding, easily found by keying '***diwali***' into your favourite search engine. You may also find this particular website helpful: http://www.diwalifestival.org.

US Thanksgiving – late November

Thanksgiving in the US is celebrated on the 4th Thursday of November, which tends to get rolled into a very long weekend which creates a few irritations particularly amongst widely dispersed families who may find it difficult — and expensive — to travel home for both this and Christmas which takes place a mere four weeks or so later. However this is not our problem.

In all honesty there is very little difference in theme terms between Canadian Thanksgiving (see above) and the US version, other than the dates involved. Decorations are still focused on autumnal flora and the menu is virtually iden-tical to that of the Canadians, although there is a fascinating, additional historical element to American Thanksgiving menus which you might find very interesting (see Chapter 6).

What the US Thanksgiving does afford you, though, is the excuse to use its concepts as a wedding theme rather later in the autumn.

St Andrew's Day – 30 November

St Andrews Day has only become a public holiday in Scotland in relatively recent times, although it has been celebrated privately for some years.

I don't need to tell you that wedding themes along these lines involve bright tartans, roaring fires, Scottish music (and preferably Scottish dancing after dinner) along with a wide variety of tasty treats (see Chapter 6).

Unlike Burns' Night, where you are pretty much restricted in both cultural and culinary terms, St Andrew's Day allows you to celebrate everything Scottish whether connect with Burns or not. Ceilidh dancing, in particular, is something you may want to include in your itinerary.

Autumn or winter weddings often remove the advantage of being outside; however, this should not be discounted. With the light fading fast you can take advantage by decorating the outside of your venue with an abundance of fairy lights, or choose a feature, trees or a statue and add up lighters in your chosen colour. Guide your guests into your venue with a walkway of lit torches or storm lanterns, let the magic begin.

If you have windows at your venue, some simple decoration outside adds to the atmosphere and may be as simple as lanterns made from tea lights in jam jars.

Christmas conjures up images of reds, greens and gold, or alternatively go for the ultimate in contemporary; choose white and silver, understatement at its best. Why not adorn your venue in white muslin, back lit to create your very own ice palace.

What about giant gypsophila balls suspended from the ceiling by your chosen colour ribbon, giving a very contemporary effect of giant snowballs, or add lights and coloured flowers and diamantes giving the affect of giant baubles.

Don't eliminate the good old Christmas tree; with a bit of imagination it can be easily transformed. Fill it with fairy lights, lots of is a must, and add feathers or black and white photographs of your guests. A delicious scent will cap it all; Christmas conjures up cinnamon, or try vanilla for a contemporary twist.

Emma Marygold
Marygold Weddings
http://www.marygoldweddings.com

General winter themes

Now we have moved on into the truly chilly months in the northern hemisphere, and especially in northern Europe, we need to take a realistic look at what options there are for wedding themes that can lighten and brighten us up. Never fear; dark and damp though things may look, there is much to inspire us.

> ... go to town on lighting and create mood. Use lighting to vary the reception, low lighting for the drinks reception, pinspotting on the dining tables, gobos for the dance area. Trees with p lights look gorgeous. Be adventurous with your colour scheme, somehow you are less dictated to by the colour scheme of the room you are in when it is dark and you can use just ambient lighting.
>
> **Siobhan Craven-Robins**
> **From This Day Forward**
> **www.fromthisdayforward.co.uk**

Après ski theme

Some very good friends of mine hold a party in southern England every November (late November) to celebrate their birthday. They are both ski fanatics, but of course outdoor skiing is not exactly a commonplace sport here in leafy Bedfordshire. Nonetheless, this intrepid pair organize a party where guests dress in après ski gear, eat not only barbecued food but also lovely Alpine fondues, listen to folk music from the mountains the world over, and generally have a wonderful time.

And all of this takes place outdoors, in their garden in southern England. Despite it being late November in temperatures that range from freezing up to 10°C max, and possibly in the rain.

Crazy British idiots? Quite possibly, but these parties have been going on for several years and we guests all enjoy them.

Now I'm not suggesting that your wedding theme should take this route. But, if you might have wanted your wedding to take place in a ski resort – or, if you intend to go to a ski resort for your honeymoon – this theme might just be ideal.

Think relaxed, comfortable après ski clothes ... sexy, woolly tops, ski pants or leggings, snow boots ... and a delightful atmosphere by a roaring open fire, with tables set for a tasty meat or cheese fondue. I haven't included menu ideas for fondues in Chapter 6 because that, in all probability, is a relatively remote option for you to consider.

However if this idea appeals to you, key either '**cheese fondue**' '**fondue bourguignonne**' or even '**fondue chinoise**' (a lighter and more delicate fondue option that has nothing whatsoever to do with winter!) into your favourite search engine.

And as for entertainment ... think Alpine music, folk music from the UK or any-where else that's a relevant place for you and of course, yodelling, thigh-slapping Austrian music, plus – should you really want to take things to the limit – a choice of the delicious, if viciously strong Schnapps drinks from those lofty Alpine countries.

Winter Wonderlands

As you can imagine, the Winter Wonderland theme is by far the most popular for weddings at this time of the year, and ideas for how to use it are abundant.

For the perfect 'winter wonderland' theme go white! White teamed with fairy lights, and crystals will give you a very modern but wintery feel to the day. If going for this look ensure that you use white and not ivory or off white. A crystal bouquet rather than floral can look amazing with this theme.

Bare trees wrapped in lights look amazing, no matter what your colour theme. Other colours which are great in the winter are deep reds and greens, and also golds. If it is a winter theme you want but can't afford to/don't want to travel to Lapland for your big day, a number of companies offer things such as fake snow etc to help give your wedding that winter 'wow' factor. Use candles as lighting on your tables. This will add warmth and romance to the reception.

Tara Nix
TDN Events
http://www.tdnevents.com

Topiary

Topiary can be not only effective, but also a very 'green' alternative to flowers or other pre-cut foliage decorations. As I'm sure you know, these are shrubs and bushes which have been pruned into a wild variety of shapes ... from simple balls, cones, columns and cubes to exotic birds, animals and various other objects. I quote here a list from my last weddings book, *How To Get Married In Green*:

- Aircraft
- Animals
- Bells
- Bicycles
- Birds
- Boats
- Famous buildings
- Fish
- Flowers
- Lanterns
- Urns
- Wells
- Sporting figures
- .... to name but a few.

Anyway such topiary plants, in containers, can be hired for your wedding, hence their qualifying as 'green' — they are almost endlessly reusable. And although I can't say I've witnessed this personally, I'm told that topiary shrubs adorned with lots of fairy lights and white ribbon can make the most amazing wedding theme at any time of year. Add to that some fake snow, clever lighting and perhaps a few sharply coloured baubles here and there — well, I hope that has fired up your imagination!

Cover tables with a scattering of silver sequins or stars around crystal candlesticks with white candles edged with evergreen foliage. Elsewhere, ensure fires roar in every grate, and use masses of candles and twinkly fairy lights to create a magical atmosphere.

Bridget Stott
Piece of Cake Party Planners
http://www.pieceofcakeuk.com

The Chronicles Of Narnia

This is a popular theme for winter weddings and other parties, although having been to a stage performance of 'The Lion, The Witch and The Wardrobe' I can't say the eternal winter created by the White Witch is a theme I would necessarily champion.

However, various interpretations that we've seen of the White Witch and her winter scenery are truly beautiful and looking at images thereof (key '***The Lion, The Witch and The Wardrobe***' into your favourite search engine and click on the 'images' option) you'll get some useful inspiration from the snow and ice covered trees, shrubs and other items as well as lots of sparkly ice everywhere, and of course the white fur (fake of course) adorning the characters, sleighs, etc.

Something else you may want to consider for your winter wonderland reception is an *ice sculpture*, or an *ice luge*.

You can use the natural beauty the winter months bring. Incorporate ivy, berries and even mistletoe into your bouquet, table centre and napkin decorations. Lots of fairy lights, candles, twigs and crystal create a magical feel. Carry the designs through to your stationery to tie everything together.

Emma Glen
Behind the Veil Wedding Planning Service
www.behindtheveil.co.uk

The sculptures are self-explanatory, really, and can be created to look like almost anything that would otherwise be sculpted in bronze or stone.

Ice luges, on the other hand, are not something you slide down on a sled, but blocks of ice across which vodka and other beverages are poured, so cooling them nicely while you await them on the other side of the block to receive them in a glass or even directly into your mouth. Sounds a bit messy for a wedding reception to me but ice luges are popular and they do help to break the ice .... (sorry, I'll get my coat).

For more information on these chilly artefacts, key '*ice sculptures*' into your favourite search engine.

Specific winter themes

In the paragraphs below, I have highlighted just some of our winter festivals that might be useful as themes — or if not themes, just some inspiration — for your winter wedding. Please bear in mind that I have only just touched upon ideas involving a few religions, but of course I'm aware that depending on your own culture and ethnicity there are certainly many more festivals you could observe and share in your wedding theme.

The following, then, is just a taster to get your imagination started up.

Hanukah – December

Obviously I'm aware that many Jewish weddings follow very traditional paths at whatever time of year they take place, but to me – a mere *shiksa* – the whole Hanukah story and ethos is just a wonderful basis for a delightful wedding celebration.

Whether you're Jewish or not, Hanukah is a lovely theme which you can use to whatever extent you want ... even if it's only the incorporation of those delicious latkes and many other tasty delicacies into your wedding menu (see Chapter 6).

As you probably know, Hanukah is a festival of lights beginning on the 25th day of Kislev (Hebrew month). However, on the Western calendar the actual date varies, although it's most likely to occur in December. Obviously if you are Jewish you will know the story of Hanukah, and if you don't, far be it for me to be so patronizing as to relate it here. For that information key **'Hanukah'** into your favourite search engine.

Some of the key celebrations of Hanukah include the exchange of gifts over the eight-day period – a Jewish holiday – and eating fried foods. (Bad for the waistline but so appetising.) In addition there are many decorations you (and especially your children) can make to adorn a wedding venue, so as I mention above look Hanukah up on the internet.

And finally, I understand that traditionally Hanukah is the only time of the year when Jewish people are free to gamble. So should you want to have a 'casino' theme for your wedding reception, this would be the time to do it!

Christmas – 25 December

As you know, Christmas is the Christian festivity that is celebrated in many countries worldwide. Not many people in Western countries are unaware of this festival's traditions, stories, colours, decorations and so-on, so it would probably be a bit much for me to go into great detail here about holly, mistletoe, coloured baubles, Christmas trees and the like.

As I've mentioned elsewhere, having a Christmas wedding can allow you to capitalize on the decorations already in place in churches and reception venues, so cutting back on the need for you to go to as much trouble and expense as you might otherwise. You can build on those basic decorations, too, adding extra foliage, lighting and colours.

You can even carry the theme through to your menu (see Chapter 6) and to your wedding outfits — there's nothing like a touch of bright red Santa Claus inspired hooded cloaks and fake fur wraps to give a lovely glow to the traditional wedding colours. Child attendants can be dressed as Santa's elves; the groom, best man and ushers can wear Christmas tinsel buttonholes; wedding favours can be wrapped in Christmas paper with colourful bows and placed alongside themed crackers; and even your wedding stationery can be themed with a Christmas look.

You can also consider a 'Victorian Christmas' theme with Victorian-style outfits for the bridal party and a richly decorated, candlelit reception serving some Victorian Christmas delicacies (see Chapter 6).

If you are getting married at Christmas make sure you have your paperwork to the registrar in plenty of time before the wedding as the offices will be closed over Christmas and New Year which will cause a delay with it being processed. This is particularly the case for non-UK residents as there is additional paperwork you need to obtain from your country as well.

Emma Glen
Behind the Veil Wedding Planning Service
www.behindtheveil.co.uk

New Year's Eve/New Year's Day/ Hogmanay – 31 December–2 January

New Year does not have as much to offer in terms of a wedding theme other than the sheer act of celebrating a new year and a new chapter in life — quite appropriate for a marriage!

If you're getting married in Scotland, the festivities go on for at least two days which gives you a larger 'window' into which to plan your wedding. Elsewhere the holiday is simply the one day, on 1 January.

As I suggested above, a New Year theme doesn't restrict you to as much as a Christmas or even Valentine's theme. At New Year, as long as you have plenty of celebratory bubbly, the singing of Auld Lang Syne at midnight on 31 December, plenty of party hats, noise makers, paper streamers and preferably some fireworks you can admire from the doors and windows, you're all set.

It's a great excuse for a party!

Pantomimes

As you know the Christmas and New Year period is the season for pantomimes in the UK. If you want to go 'A list' like the celebs do, you could theme your wedding around your favourite panto, complete with decorations and costumes. Alternatively you could have a theatrical theme with strong stage lighting and various 'sets' representing different pantos, perhaps sprinkled with sparkle and fairy lights, and get guests to come along dressed as their own favourite pantomime character. (You can hire such sets – key '**theatrical set hire**' into your favourite search engine.)

For your reference, here are some commonly performed pantomimes:

- Puss In Boots
- Dick Whittington
- Jack and the Beanstalk
- Peter Pan
- Aladdin
- Cinderella
- Sleeping Beauty
- Snow White and the Seven Dwarfs
- Beauty and the Beast

Burns Night — 25 January

Burns Night festivities can be anything from an informal gathering where you just pay lip service to the man here and there, right through to a large, formal occasion where you go through the entire ritual to the ninth place of decimal in detail. However, no matter how much of fan you are of Robert Burns, you may not want to replicate the whole ritual in full for your wedding reception or dinner! For your information I have summarized the procedure, so you can choose what to use at your leisure.

The *Opening Address* is given by the host — in your case, perhaps the bride's father, the best man, or the groom? Guests are welcomed and then the 'Selkirk Grace' is said:

> *Some hae meat and canna eat,*
> *and some wad eat that want it,*
> *but we hae meat and we can eat,*
> *and sae the Lord be thankit.*

When the time comes for the main course, we get into the most solemn part of the ceremony. A piper enters the room, playing appropriate music, followed by the head chef who carries the haggis (only one, but there will be plenty more for everyone in the kitchen) to the top table, which in this case would be to the bride and groom.

At this point the same person who said grace gives the *Address To The Haggis*, which consists of Burns' poem 'To A Haggis':

> *Fair fa' your honest, sonsie face,*
> *Great chieftain o' the pudding-race!*
> *Aboon them a'yet tak your place,*
> *Painch, tripe, or thairm:*
> *Weel are ye wordy o'a grace*
> *As lang's my arm.*

The groaning trencher there ye fill,
Your hurdies like a distant hill,
Your pin was help to mend a mill
In time o'need,
While thro' your pores the dews distil
Like amber bead.

His knife see rustic Labour dight,
**An' cut you up wi' ready sleight,
Trenching your gushing entrails bright,
Like ony ditch;
And then, O what a glorious sight,
Warm-reekin', rich!

Then, horn for horn, they stretch an' strive:
Deil tak the hindmost! on they drive,
Till a' their weel-swall'd kytes belyve
Are bent like drums;
Then auld Guidman, maist like to rive,
Bethankit! hums.

Is there that owre his French ragout
Or olio that wad staw a sow,
Or fricassee wad make her spew
Wi' perfect sconner,
Looks down wi' sneering, scornfu' view
On sic a dinner?

Poor devil! see him owre his trash,
As feckles as wither'd rash,
His spindle shank, a guid whip-lash;
His nieve a nit;
Thro' blody flood or field to dash,
O how unfit!

But mark the Rustic, haggis-fed,
The trembling earth resounds his tread.
Clap in his walie nieve a blade,
He'll mak it whissle;
An' legs an' arms, an' hands will sned,
Like taps o' trissle.

Ye Pow'rs, wha mak mankind your care,
And dish them out their bill o' fare,
Auld Scotland wants nae skinking ware
That jaups in luggies;
But, if ye wish her gratefu' prayer
Gie her a haggis!

No matter how good the host's memory and Scottish pronunciation might be, I strongly recommend that he or she copies this poem from one of the many websites which supply it, prints it out in big bold type and reads it — especially as by this time the odd drop or two of whisky may have been consumed.

When the host gets to the line marked above, 'An' cut you up wi' ready slight', this is the cue for the haggis the be cut open with a grand flourish, ready for serving. After the address is finished everyone claps, then stands and toasts the haggis, with whisky.

After the meal a special guest is asked to give the *Immortal Memory*, which is a short speech about Robert Burns and is considered a great honour for who-ever has been invited to say it. This is where you might want to deviate from the Burns Night ritual and turn things back into a wedding reception, espe-cially as the traditional Burns Night procedure from here on is very similar to the speeches and toasts of a traditional wedding anyway.

There is no set script for the Immortal Memory, which means that the person concerned has to compose it him or herself. This can actually take a lot of work. If you do decide the replace this with the father of the bride's speech, thankfully there are some good books around from How to Books to help you. The Immortal Memory ends with the line, 'to the immortal memory of Robert

Burns', or with the first of the bridal toasts. The father of the bride – if he's a good Scot – might even combine the two.

Next on the Burns Night list is the *Toast to the Lassies*, which less serious and can be humorous – rather like the Best Man's Speech. However, next in the traditional wedding ritual is the groom's speech here. Let's not let that small discrepancy make a difference.

Finally in the Burns Night ritual is the *Response to the Toast to the Lassies* which, considering that Burns lived in the latter part of the 18th century shows a remarkably modern attitude to women giving speeches. I'm all for that (but then I did write *Wedding Speeches For Women* for How To Books). With some readjustment here and there you could work your own speeches so that the bride, and/or chief bridesmaid, responds to the Best Man's speech. And with the Scottish and Burns connections there are ample opportunities for humour, comparisons, metaphors and even pathos.

On a traditional Burns Night the guests continue through the evening singing songs and listening to poems, but here you might like to bend the Burns rules and get going with some Scottish dancing. And to round off the evening, you'll enjoy a rousing chorus of 'Auld Lang Syne', the words of which were, of course, written by Robert Burns.

Valentines Day – 14 February

The theming of a Valentine's Day wedding is pretty well known – hearts, roses, all things red, cupids, aphrodisiac foods (see Chapter 6) and chocolate ... how about a chocolate fountain?

You might even want to consider theming around old movies and love stories ... anything from Adam and Eve to Anthony and Cleopatra to Romeo and Juliet to Queen Victoria and Prince Albert to Lauren Bacall and Humphrey Bogart to Elizabeth Taylor and Richard Burton, although that last couple did not end up in everlasting matrimonial bliss. However neither did Romeo and Juliet, yet their story represents romance probably more than any other.

You can really emphasize the romantic theme with your entertainment and music. During dinner, you could have a violinist or two circulating around the tables, serenading the ladies with sweet sounds — and you can get your band or DJ to play music by some of our most romantic singers like Frank Sinatra, Tony Bennett, Roberta Flack etc. or if you want more contemporary romantic vocalists, try Michael Bublé, Sadé or Jacqui Dankworth.

One thing you may want to guard against is overdoing the Valentine's Day theme. You can have too much of hearts, roses, cupid bows and red absolutely everywhere. This then takes attention away from the bride and groom, and the real reason why you're there! Use your common sense and creativity to enhance your bridal look, ceremony and reception with the classic Valentine's decor. A moderate amount of such theming is, if anything, more powerful — and certainly more effective.

General spring themes

Spring themes obviously centre around the emerging new flora and fauna, especially with the early spring flowers like snowdrops, crocus, daffodils, primroses, tulips and so-on. Colours need to be light but strong, too (save the sweet pea pastels for a summer wedding) like pinks, yellows and bright greens.

Specific spring themes

Particularly in the case of St David's Day and Easter, the key elements and symbols used for the specific festivals can actually be used to represent more general spring themes — daffodils being a good example.

Here are a few specific themes, though, that you may well want to consider.

St David's Day – 1 March

If you're Welsh or have Welsh connections, this could be the theme for you if you're getting married around this time. Not only do daffodils form a key part of the theme, but also leeks, which happily can be incorporated into your menu (See Chapter 6.)

St David's Day celebrations in themselves usually involve eating and singing, which are extremely pleasant elements to incorporate into your wedding. You may not want to go so far as to put yourselves or the bridal attendants into traditional Welsh costume, but certainly elements of it could be incorporated, e.g. petticoats and frilled white bonnets for the young girls, plus white shirt, jabot, waistcoat and breeches for the young boys.

Beautiful choral music, of course, is a very important part of Welsh culture – so how about a Welsh choir to sing at your ceremony and/or reception?

St Patrick's Day – 17 March

Think green, green, green! This is the colour of St Patrick's Day although funnily enough, it hasn't always been green. In fact prior to the mid-18th century the St Patrick's colour was blue. Anyway green is a useful colour to incorporate into your wedding because it allows you to use lots of evergreen foliage (the leaves won't be out on the deciduous trees yet) as decoration.

If you are using this as a secular, rather than religious theme, then you can incorporate orange colours, too. The classic element, too, is the intrepid shamrock. Once again, in the UK at least it's likely to be too early in the season for real shamrocks, so you may have to make do with artificial ones.

The other classical elements of St Patrick's Day are the Irish food and drink (see Chapter 6) as well as Irish music and dancing.

Easter – March or April

Like Christmas and Valentine's Day, the Easter themes and traditions are very well known so I don't need to go into much detail here.

Think in terms of brightly coloured Easter eggs, chicks, baby rabbits, Easter baskets, Easter bonnets (great inspiration not just for the bridal party but also for mothers of the bride and groom and other women). Attendants can carry little Easter baskets containing flowers or Easter eggs. Wedding favours can be in the shape of eggs – e.g. coloured, handmade organic soaps, nestled in little boxes of straw.

Traditional Easter colours used to be purple and yellow, but now anything goes. Purples and yellows, however, do you give you a lot of scope for some interesting decorations as well as floral arrangements.

If you can get hold of potted primroses and primulae in these colours they will look stunning as table decorations, and guests could even take the small ones home as favours. Daffodils, as well as tulips in yellow and purple tones, make lovely larger arrangements.

St George's Day – 23 April

As I mention in Chapter 6, St George's Day is being lobbied for very strongly in some quarters, to be turned into a public holiday as is the case for St David's Day (Wales), St Patrick's Day (Ireland) and St Andrew's Day (Scotland).

Unlike those events (and probably because it has not been established as a public holiday yet) St George's doesn't have much in the way of quantifiable traditions and symbols associated with it, so as far as theming is concerned you can do pretty much whatever you like as long as it's English.

Don't forget, though, the St George's Cross and its colours of red and white, which conveniently work very well for wedding colours.

If you want to go back through history for your wedding theme, this could be a good opportunity to do it. For example, you could go for a St George and the dragon theme, or even a medieval banquet with some jousting. There are several companies in the UK who offer these medieval banquets for wedding parties – just key '***medieval weddings***' into your favourite search engine.

Alternatively you could choose a Shakespearean theme ... perhaps based on your favourite Shakespeare play, with outfits based on Elizabethan fashions and menus and drinks to match. There is some interesting further information about that idea here: http://www.william-shakespeare.info.

Non-seasonal themes suitable for the cooler months

There are endless ideas that I could include here but this chapter would then become the whole book! What I have done is to pick on some themes I think can work really well for a wedding, so either you can run with one of those or use them as inspiration for developing your own ideas.

Black and white

A black and white theme can, in theory, be used in the summer as well, but in the cooler months it can make a more dramatic statement. That's because you can use more in the way of artificial lighting to heighten the glamorous effects as well as sparkling crystals, fairy lights, fake snow, etc. which aren't appropriate in the summer. This theme is a favourite amongst celebrities who either dress the entire bridal party in black and white, or alternatively get all the guests to wear black and/or white, and then make themselves and their attendants really stand out against that backdrop in bright, eye-catching colours.

1920s

The 'roaring twenties' weren't called that for nothing. This was the decade when people really were kicking up their heels in Europe and North America after the horrors of WW1, and before the harsh realities of the coming depression in the 1930s had raised its ugly head. Flapper outfits were sexy and cute – wedding dresses of the day were very flattering – and some of their music and dances like the Charleston and the jitterbug made rock 'n' roll jiving look positively tame. It is ideal if your venue is 'Art Deco' in style.

1940s

The 1940s do not hold happy memories for everyone still around to tell the tale, as WW2 ravaged much of Europe and elsewhere. However, the second half of the decade saw people enjoying life again with glamorous satin and silk gowns – very flattering styles for a wedding outfit – plus romantic big band music that everyone still loves to dance to today.

1950s

This one is perfect for the rockers! Ducktail haircuts and winkle picker shoes for the boys, prom dresses, crinolines and soft curls for the girls, American diner style food and drink and as much rock 'n' roll as you can handle. This theme can be a wild one, but even granny will remember her jiving days and show you young folks how to do it at your reception.

1960s

Even if you or your parents do not have a fondness for the Beatles, the 1960s was one of the most interesting decades in recent times in terms of other music and of course, fashion. Think Twiggy, Mary Quant, mini dresses and flat shoes or 'kinky' boots, long hair and big eyes, collarless suit jackets for the boys. Or if you prefer the latter part of that decade, go for the hippy/flower power look — beautiful long floaty dresses, endless love beads, floral shirts for the guys, and flowers, flowers everywhere; plus some of the best music of the 20th century whether it's the Mersey sound of the UK or the emerging Tamla Motown sound from the USA.

1980s

This was the era of the big hair and huge padded shoulders — power dressing at its best. It's a style that's very well suited for a magnificent wedding dress and bridesmaids' outfits that echo the theme. You can also have a great time developing a New Romantics theme across your clothes, makeup and hair as well as your decorations — all Vivienne Westwood with kooky makeup, platform shoes, long gloves and a wild hot potch of elegance mixed with eccentricity. Music of the day is still very listenable to today, with some classic stuff having been produced by bands like Spandau Ballet, Duran Duran, and of course, ABBA!

Sports

A sports theme will only really work if both bride and groom are equally committed players or fans, but when this is the case it can give your wedding a truly unique touch. How far you take things is entirely up to you; it could be that you simply incorporate your team's colours as the main focus of your wedding scheme, or you can go the whole hog and adorn everywhere — and everyone — with appropriate badged and coloured accessories and decorations. Think beyond the usual team sports and other recreations, too; you can do a lot within a theme with ideas from the worlds of golf, equestrianism/horse racing, tennis, motor racing, belly dancing (think Arabian nights), judo/karate, etc.

Eastern splendour

Oriental themes aren't hard to put together and can look stunning, with clothes based on anything from saris to kimonos, strong primary colours, minimalist decor and of course, a menu to match — or perhaps 'fusion' cuisine across more than one Eastern culture. If you choose Japanese, bonsai trees make fabulous table decorations especially if illuminated with tiny fairy lights — and they're a green option, as they can be hired or bought and given to guests as wedding favours.

Monte Carlo evening

This is a useful theme because the decor, backdrop and entertainment are all part and parcel of the same thing. The men need to wear tuxedos and the women, long evening dresses. Cards and dice can be represented across wedding stationery and various other incarnations. Drinks should be champagne or sophisticated cocktails. And if you don't want people to lose their own shirts, guests can be given a pile of 'chips' as wedding favours to use at gambling tables after the formalities. There are numerous organisations in the UK who offer a package deal for casino parties — key '**casino evenings**' into your favourite search engine.

Country and Western

In all honesty this theme is easier to put together in the summer, because you can used an unheated barn for your reception. But if you and your intended are dedicated country and/or folk music fans, there is still no reason why you can't decorate a heated, indoor venue with rustic items, a few bales of hay or straw, pitchforks, barrows, even a small pony cart or hand cart, and so-on to make it look like the inside of a barn. Your clothes will be informal, obviously, and if you're going for the western end of things then cowboy/cowgirl outfits are crucial! If the venue is big enough you can have a full scale barn dance, but if there isn't room for that you can still consider line dancing — an ideal entertainment for a wedding because everyone from small children to grannies can join in. Music can range from electric Country and Western to fiddle and accordion groups to ceilidh bands.

4 Picking clothes, accessories, beauty

When thinking about this chapter in the broadest possible sense I had two initial reactions: one, for people getting married in the northern hemisphere, wrap up warmly, and two, for people travelling to exotic, warmer locations, do not wrap up warmly.

It's not a simple as that. Or as relevant.

Let's start with the cooler options.

Wedding attire for cold weather

Although there's no question that getting married in the cooler months — especially when you're talking snowy and/or icy environs — necessitates some pretty warm clothes to ensure you get to your ceremony and reception and back without being afflicted by frostbite.

However, bear in mind that unless you're (a) raving mad or (b) getting married in an 'ice hotel' or similar venue (see Part 2) once you combat the raging storms outdoors you will eventually land somewhere relatively warm and comfortable. That's where a clever choice of wardrobe is called for.

Layers, layers, layers

When I say 'clever choice,' what I really mean is 'practical choice'. In other words, allow for layers. Instead of hoping that the weather will be pleasing enough to let you get from car to ceremony to reception in a strapless gown before you have time to be refrigerated (and believe me, many brides do think they'll get away with this — and don't), plan on including a cute bolero or shrug to top your wedding dress, and if necessary a sexy, furry (well, faux furry) cape on top. Such capes can look absolutely stunning and provide a co-ordinated added dimension to your overall look.

On a more practical level what this permits is the option for you to be photographed going into and out of your ceremony and reception without exposing blue noses and goose bumps to the camera, should weather conditions permit outdoor photography.

Not just layers for you

Obviously you will need to carry through this thinking to the rest of your bridal party, too. Bridesmaids shivering in skimpy dresses will (a) look bad in the pictures and (b) probably never speak to you again if they have to endure anything but a fleeting exposure to the elements en route to your nice, warm reception. Children as bridal attendants may not complain about the cold, but their parents certainly will if, a couple of days after your cold-weather wedding, the little ones come down with the sniffles or worse due to 'catching a chill' on the day. So some warm – but removable – layers of clothing are essential all round.

If you decide on strapless, sleeveless or short-sleeved styles for you and the bridesmaids, consider long gloves for the outdoors bits – so elegant, and warmer than nothing. And boleros, shrugs, capes etc. look just as good on bridesmaids as they do on the bride.

You could even consider carrying decorative hand muffs instead of bouquets, and if appropriate, don't forget to incorporate warm tights into the outfits.

What about the men?

Men's clothing tends to be warmer than women's which is a distinct advantage in this case, but don't forget that the fabrics used in men's clothing are not necessarily draught-proof. So in particularly chilly circumstances, you might like to suggest – politely – some warm underwear, or at least outer layers, for the guys, too.

If they are wearing smart suits or tuxedos/dinner jackets/morning suits, they may like to consider wearing waistcoats rather than 'cummerbunds' as waist-coats will provide them with more insulation from cold in draughty churches or other wedding ceremony venues. Once safely at the reception venue, men in waistcoats with jackets removed do tend to look somewhat better than men with shirts and cummerbunds, if only because you don't get the shirts floating up around their middles.

Ordinary suits can, of course, be of heavier material than those you'd chose in the summer months, but beware of over-heating here. Once again, jackets and waistcoats can provide adequate insulation from the cold outside — but offer the convenient option of being discardable once warmth is eventually found.

Some more thoughts on winter wedding clothes

If you're getting married in potentially wet and/or muddy circumstances, you might well like to consider the length of your wedding dress, and whether or not a train is necessary — or at least, if a train can be 'bustled' to a height above ground level. Ditto for the bridesmaids' dresses assuming they're full length.

That's because no matter how careful you are to hitch up your skirts as you tiptoe through the rainy, muddy church yard or outdoor surroundings of any type of wedding venue, something may distract you, you let go, and you could finish up with unpleasant brownish stains around your hem. Hemlines that are a couple of centimetres above ground level (with shoes on) will stay above all but the most pesky of puddles and continue looking good through-out the day.

There are more colours than just white

Although traditional white can look fantastic in strong summer light, in colder months it can tend to look a bit washy and disappear into the background. For an autumn, winter or early spring wedding you might find that a rich, darker variant works far better; cream, gold, pale pink, pale blue, silver or even a non-traditional colour.

Particularly if you are not having a traditional (i.e. 'white' wedding) you really can choose whatever colour scheme takes your fancy, and bearing in mind that weddings during these months can be affected by dull, darkish weather some vibrant colours and fashion statements will go a long way towards compensating for the lack of light and warmth.

Look towards India for inspiration

Whether you're Indian or not, you could take a leaf out of the Indian weddings 'book' and choose a brilliant, stunning red for your wedding dress colour. According to Indian tradition, red is the colour of happiness and good luck for the bridal couple — and certainly, it will 'warm up' your wedding look no matter how cold it is outdoors.

Tradtionally the wedding attire can take the form of the *salwar kameez* which, conveniently for a wedding in colder conditions involves elegant trousers topped by a smooth tunic. There is also the *gaghra choli,* which consists of a long skirt accompanied by a shortish top — also a comforting idea for cold weather nuptials, although in true Indian tradition the top is that short that it exposes your midriff, which could be draughty.

In addition, of course there is the very traditional sari which can look unbelievably elegant on women of all nationalities. An example of how delightful this style is could be seen when (British) actress Elizabeth Hurley married (Indian) Arun Nayar in 2007. Although she wore a traditional Western European style at the UK version of their wedding, for the Indian ceremony her vibrant, jewel-encrusted *sari* frankly left her UK 'meringue' dress way behind in elegance terms. At least that's my opinion.

Accompanying these options is often a scarf called a *dupatta*. Not only would this be conveniently warm and cosy, but also can be very elegant — and obviate the need for a head-dress, veil, etc.

In true Indian tradition, fabrics and designs for such wedding attire are incredibly elaborate, ornate, and beautiful. Stunning embroidery, jewels and crystals and even silver and gold adornments can be incorporated into the fabrics — mostly commonly satins and chiffons. Yet the cost involved need not be ridiculous; in fact if you shop around either within your local Indian community or on the internet, you should be able to commission some wonderful bridal and bridesmaids outfits for rather less than you might think.

For an online search, key '**Indian wedding dresses**' into your favourite search engine.

What about warmer fabrics?

Warmer fabrics are a great idea for cold weather wedding attire, but there is a 'but' here as I suggested above. That is, quite simply, that despite the weather outdoors being cold, damp – snowy, even – and otherwise unfriendly, in our modern day and age there's a good chance that your ceremony venue (and especially your reception venue) will offer the delightfully modern benefit of good central heating.

Okay, if you're getting married in a tiny chapel on a blustery hillside followed by a reception in an ancient castle in a remote hamlet, you may well need to wear warm fabrics plus woolly knickers and lots more besides. But let's get real here. Even in the remoter parts of the UK and elsewhere in northern hemispheres, there aren't many places now that have the gall to offer themselves as wedding venues without decent heating, unless they're ice hotels (see Part 2).

So, that could possibly affect your decisions about the weight of the fabrics you choose for your wedding dress, and the clothes of your bridesmaids and other attendants. However, having said all that I personally love the heavier fabrics because they look and feel so good ... satin, velvet, crèpe, moiré, brocade, taffeta ... the list goes on.

As I mentioned earlier in this chapter, think layers; if you want to indulge in a dress or outfit in a heavier fabric, ensure that you can remove layers as necessary from shivery outdoor temperatures, through to the steamy climes of the dance floor.

What about the children?

Children's clothes become quite an issue, especially if – as is often the case the little ones are key parts of the bridal party and ceremony.

As you will already know if you have children, when they are feeling (a) cold and (b) a little bit intimidated by the formality of a parent's or other close relative's wedding, they can become very negative indeed. Although there's not much you can do to lessen the stress caused by the nature of the occasion, you can at least ensure that things are not made worse by the fact that they are cold and shivery at any point.

Once again, layers are key here, especially when you think that once the kids get to the reception and begin to run around they will cast aside all but strictly necessary clothing in their enthusiasm for the occasion.

Junior bridesmaids can, of course, be provided with shrugs, boleros and capes similar to those worn by the grownups. And small pages can be dressed (a) in long trousers rather than shorts and (b) with layers that will keep them warm, too, and enable them to peel off as they warm up later.

As for style? There's nothing little kids like more than 'dressing up' in winter wonderland outfits, especially if they're fans of winter wonderland scenes from 'The Chronicles of Narnia' or similar fantasies. See Chapter 3 for more on that. Just make sure that the layers can be peeled off easily.

And for the mothers of the bride and groom?

Happily the mums are far less restricted in what they can wear and although basically the same principles apply — more, lighter layers rather than fewer, heavier layers — cool weather weddings offer them the opportunity to be rather more dramatic in their fashion statements than in the warmer months. Although the fabrics they choose for their outfits may not be that heavy, the dimmer light of autumn, winter and spring just begs for powerful colours and strong designs that will light up their corners of the occasion.

Mums can go berserk with faux fur and extravagant fluffy, warm-looking items if that's what they prefer and look best in. In contrast, for women who prefer a classical look, these times of the year are perfect for a stunningly simple, tailored look in crisp, medium-weight fabric in a mysteriously dark colour — perhaps set off by an outrageous 'fascinator' or other exotic accessory.

Jewellery

Accessorizing a winter wedding outfit should follow the slightly heavier, more dramatic look that the bride's dress and outfits of the bridesmaids and mums of the bride/groom will inspire.

Obviously if you're going for a Winter Wonderland look, then silver jewellery and snowy-white and silver tiaras or head-dresses are just perfect.

However, should you be choosing richer, deeper colours and tones, then this should be reflected in the jewellery and other accessories you wear. A deep cream brocade wedding dress, for example, will not be adequately complemented by a fine silver and crystal pendant or necklace. You need to balance the power of the dress with some stronger jewellery – in this case, perhaps a string of larger, cream-coloured pearls with matching drop earrings.

If you're choosing to be inspired by Indian wedding attire then you will have a wonderful choice of Indian jewellery which, as you know, is incredibly glamorous, colourful and flattering.

The style and drama of the bridesmaids outfits need similarly to be reflected in and balanced by their jewellery. Unless they are going to be in light coloured, light-weight fabrics, the jewellery will need to make a stronger statement in terms of either size, colour, or both.

Tiaras and headwear

Once again, these need to complement the rest of your outfit. If your dress and cape suggest a scene from Narnia, a delicate tiara or headpiece just won't work. Instead, choose a hood on your cape that frames your head with luxuriant faux fur and rich fabrics ... dropping to reveal a sleek, sophisticated up-do underneath.

If your outfit is to be brightly coloured and based – perhaps – on Indian or other non-UK influences, take a leaf from those cultures' book and wear something appropriately exotic on your head. Indian culture, in particular, offers some sensational ideas for this, combining head-wear with jewellery that continues down your face and body.

Footwear

Here's where we need to get boring for a bit and think about the realities of northern hemisphere weddings in the autumn, winter and spring. Whether we like it or not, these times can be wet — and more invasively wet than the summer days when you get a shower or two. And that's before you begin to consider the cold factor.

Have no fear. Provided that you plan appropriately your wedding footwear not only can be water-resistant, but also warm as well.

One very sensible option is to go for wedding boots — typically, wedding boots of the old Victorian style which are quite easily available. They're comfortable, wearable, and should they poke out from under your dress, look lovely. For more on that, key '*Victorian wedding boots*' into your favourite search engine.

Naturally not everyone wants to wear boots and shoes are the next consideration. Although it should go without saying, strappy, sandal-type shoes for the bride, bridesmaids and mums are probably a bad idea unless you all are prepared to stuff those in a bag ready to slide into at the reception, having left at the door your more sensible options.

But what if a change of shoe isn't possible?

Take the sensible route.

Go for a closed shoe made from leather or even a synthetic material. The latter is less likely to absorb moisture if it's raining out, but equally less likely to be 'breathable' for your poor, aching feet at the end of the day. However, either of these variants is likely to result in somewhat less wet feet for you — and for your bridal party — should you all have to traipse through sodden circumstances.

If you are going to wear the same shoes or boots throughout the day, it's well worth spraying them beforehand with your preferred brand of leather or fabric protector, to give them the best possible chance of surviving the day unscathed.

In your shoes (oh, *please!*) I would do the following — select shoes or boots for the parts of your wedding where you will need to enter, leave and/or walk around outdoors, but also choose shoes you'll be happy to wear for the reception into which you can change when you're sure that no further outdoor participation is required.

This may well mean that you have a change of shoes when you get to the reception. But with a little forward planning and organisation that shouldn't be difficult — and will be well worth it.

Makeup: cool climate

In cooler, darker circumstances you will want to ensure your makeup and that of your bridesmaids carries sufficient drama and statement to support — and even enhance the prevailing light conditions.

Makeup artists insist that the light levels outdoors when you're getting married have an influence on how you should target your makeup and that of the other key members of the bridal party. In the northern hemisphere in the cooler months, for a daytime weddings it's safe to assume that natural daylight is going to be pretty soft. So a natural look is very important; anything heavy will look over-stated and too dramatic.

If your northern hemisphere wedding takes place in the evening, however, you can take a much more dramatic approach because artificial light demands strong colours, shades and contrasts. By all means go wild with your makeup in these circumstances, but don't forget that (a) your makeup is likely to have to last for some hours on the day and (b) despite it being cold outside you're likely to get warm and maybe even perspire a bit.

So make allowances for that and ensure that your emergency kit bag contains the right ingredients for a touch up, or if necessary a major rework:

- Face wipes
- Makeup remover
- Moisturiser
- Foundation
- Powder or de-shiner

- Mascara
- Eye shadow
- Eye liner
- Eyelash glue (if you're wearing false eyelashes)
- Lip brush and liner
- Lipstick
- (and of course, brush, comb and hairspray).

Now ... what about what to wear in hot climates?

To a very large extent this is going to be dictated by where you're going and what it's going to be like there. Hardly rocket science.

However, if you haven't been to exotic tropical or sub-tropical climates before, it's worth thinking about this a little further. Although these places look stunning in pictures and videos and in all honesty are just stunning and beautiful, what many people forget here is that, along with the high temperatures, humidity can be high, too.

Not that this should put you off. However, should you by any chance be contemplating going out to such an exotic location for your wedding in clothes that don't quite work in such climates, you could be buying into a somewhat uncomfortable experience.

Cool clothes, cool fabrics

High humidity means that whatever you wear needs to be 'breathable' – in other words, allowing your body to do its thing without the inconvenient barrier to ventilation that some 'manmade' fabrics put forward.

The key here is to choose clothing made from natural fabrics – they are the most 'breathable' and forgiving in a hot, humid climate – plus of course, fabrics that are light and airy.

If you're bringing your wedding dress from the UK, make sure it's made from a fabric that's as crush-proof as possible. Obviously, unless you're wedding is to take place in a very remote location, wherever you go you're likely to find the options of an iron and an ironing board. But don't count on this notion too much.

Another important consideration is the fact that we northern hemisphere people do swell up a bit in hot climates — all to do with fluid retention, etc. So do make allowances for that if you're having your wedding outfit made in the (chilly) UK and then importing it into the country where your wedding is going to be.

What else matters for a beach weddding?

For a start, wedding clothes in white. In hot, steamy climates white is a very good colour as it helps to reflect the sun, thereby keeping you cooler, which is especially important if you're getting married on a very hot beach in an exotic location.

Avoid extra-long full length dresses, as these are likely to get trashed on a beach and may well make walking difficult for you and the other girls in your wedding party.

Also avoid wearing heeled shoes for a beach wedding. For any of you who can't see why this is a bad idea, think sand and heels disappearing there into! However, unless you really are a wild child it probably isn't a good idea to go barefoot. Many of the most glamorous beaches in the world contain highly undesirable materials, insects, etc., that personally I wouldn't want to step on. But then maybe I'm just an unromantic old trout.

> ... the couple should pay attention to the weather and wear sunscreen prior to the wedding and on the wedding day. This is to avoid to turning up at their wedding burnt and/or with tan lines (horrible ... we saw so many brides making this mistake over and over again).
>
> **Deborah Taliani**
> **Just get Married! Wedding Planners**
> **www.justgetmarried.com**

Makeup: warm climate

If you have ever spent time in tropical or sub-tropical climates you will know just how pointless it is to attempt a full makeup in temperatures much above about 30°C. What happens is that it melts, streaks, clumps, congeals, and makes you feel about as glamorous as an ice-cream at a barbecue.

Many makeup artists and other gurus will tell you not to worry, that with this product or that product you can overcome the melting makeup and ultra-shine factors. In my experience, to a limited extent these claims might be true, but at the end of the day a more considered approach is probably best.

In other words, trust your instincts. And in hot (and particularly humid) circumstances forget all the makeup recommendations you might get from glossy magazines. Looking good in these circumstances is about glowing and beaming your happiness through. Let your makeup reflect that, as simply as possible, and above all avoid cluttering that with products and 'stuff' that merely gets in the way.

If you want to look at your best for your wedding pictures, I don't need to tell you to avoid too much sun in the days before the ceremony — there's a big difference between a healthy glow and a bright red sunburn. No matter how effective your concealer or foundation is it won't cover up a sunburnt nose completely. So in all probability it's safer for you to avoid more than a little bit of sunbathing and instead go the fake tan route for the wedding itself.

As I've suggested above, in a very warm climate few people choose a very formal style of outfit, particularly as for the men a dark suit will be unbearably uncomfortable and even a heavy, structured dress will be hot and cumbersome. For similar reasons it's well worth your while to keep your hairstyle and makeup simple, unstructured and as natural as possible.

5 Organizing receptions

As we're talking about food and drink ideas in Chapter 6 and themes in Chapter 3, this chapter is a catch-all where we can look at some of the more practical considerations involved.

Car parking

Ideally, the venue of your choice will have a car park that's (a) large enough to accommodate all your guests' cars and (b) very close to the entrance of the building so guests don't have a long trek potentially in cold, wet circumstances. Often this isn't possible, though; the venue's car park may be small and offer an 'overflow' car park in a field way beyond the grounds, or if it's in a town centre, it may expect guests to find their own parking spaces wherever they can get one. Either way that's bad enough on a summer day ... but in the rain, snow, cold wind etc. it can be a nightmare.

Rather than expose your guests to such potential misery, you would do better to direct them to a large public car park as near to the reception venue as possible, and organise a 'park and ride' facility whereby they are picked up from their cars by minibus and taken to the venue that way. If your wedding is fairly small you might even get away with asking friends to volunteer to give lifts in their own MPVs ('people carriers') — but if not, you can probably do a deal with a local taxi or minibus company, or even — if appropriate — with the company that's providing transport for the bridal party.

Worst-case weather scenario?

I don't like to be a total killjoy, but if your wedding is due to take place in a part of the world where snow (or at least deep mud) is a potential issue, don't be optimistic — be pro-active.

65

Funnily enough if your wedding is taking place in a country and surroundings where snow and ice are commonplace, you don't need to worry so much – local folklore and conditions will usually permit you and your guests to have a fabulous time without worrying about two-metre snowdrifts. Even if you're not prepared for that, they are.

Where we can get into deep doo-doo – or snow, rather – is in the UK and other northern European countries where snow is a comparatively rare problem, but that can nonetheless wreak havoc should it coincide with your wedding reception.

Obviously you will know when snow is at its most likely; probably not that often in the south of the UK, but more likely in the north.

Where this really turns into a potential problem is when you have guests parking their cars in a car park or, Heaven forbid, a field, that could become snow-laden.

Solution? Ensure that you have a friendly farmer or three standing by with tractors to tow people away to safety, and also that should snow be forecast you have an appropriate snow-clearing vehicle standing by to ensure not only that wedding guests can get their cars into the venue's parking area, but also get out again afterwards ... even if that is at 02:00 the next morning.

Photographs and reception line

This can be another nightmare in less than favourable weather conditions, especially if there is a large number of guests. When people arrive at the reception they are expected to wait around while the bridal party has photographs taken, and then wait their turn to go through the reception line to offer their formal greetings and congratulations.

In the autumn, winter and spring months it's even more important than in the summer to ensure guests not only are not kept standing around for too long, but also that they are warm, dry and entertained with a glass of something – perhaps mulled wine? – and a few nibbles. I've seen guests at weddings even in midsummer getting very grumpy waiting to go through the reception line; so if you combine their lowered blood sugar levels with feeling cold and damp, you may end up with some very unhappy guests indeed.

Coats and things

In the cooler months of the year people will almost certainly arrive in coats and possibly boots, umbrellas and other bad weather gear. It's important to have somewhere near the entrance of the reception venue where they can check these items.

And it's also important — especially for the women — to have somewhere they can go and refresh their outfits, adjust their hair, hats, makeup etc. after having taken off their outer garments and possibly having battled through howling gales between transport and venue.

Don't forget that children will be wrapped up against the elements, too, so provision should be made for them.

And while we're talking about children

At summer weddings in warm circumstances, children usually love the chance to get out into the gardens/grounds of the reception venue and let rip. At least that's what my son and his cousins did at a family wedding one summer in Warwickshire — and the peacocks at that stately home venue are, I'm sure, still warning their grandchildren to stay away permanently from humans who are three feet tall or less, dressed in long gowns or sailor suits, who arrive in the grounds at 100 mph screeching and yelling.

Anyway. That's hardly an issue in the autumn, spring and winter months, but what is an issue is children's very low boredom threshold. At these colder, wetter times of the year it's important to remember that children at wedding receptions can and do get very, very bored. As you haven't got the option of sending them out into the grounds to chase the local wildlife, you may well need to ensure they have somewhere they can go — indoors — to let off steam and get away from all the grownup stuff.

Obviously that's not essential. But speaking as a parent I would heartily rec-ommend it. And the good news is that more and more reception venues are taking this message on board and are providing some helpful solutions, rather as we've seen in recent years in holiday resorts.

If there is no such option available at your chosen venue, it may well be worth your while to consider arranging something privately. You'll need to have a room set aside and beg or borrow some toys, books, games, lots of scrap paper, pencils, crayons (not permanent markers or you may be in for expensive cleanup bills from the venue) etc. And if you can't persuade some responsible adults or teenagers to supervise the children for the entire duration, an alternative is to set up a rota, with parents and teens sharing the supervisory duties in shifts of 30–60 minutes or so.

Heating

Happily the UK has been dragged kicking and screaming from the dark ages of the early 20th century when central heating was considered a new-fangled and unnecessarily expensive luxury even in hotels and especially in castles, stately homes and other venues popular for wedding receptions. Modern day brides and grooms don't buy all that 'romantic' nonsense about draughty ballrooms and banqueting halls and demand a decent level of heating and comfort.

Naturally, modern hotels and other venues offer proper climate control, so if that's your choice for your reception there's no problem. However, those old approaches to heating still lurk in venues of a more traditional, historical nature and if you're having your reception in a place like this, I would make it a priority to find out exactly how the place will be heated.

Huge, roaring open fires are beautiful and very romantic, provided they are not the only or at least the only *main* source of heat. Realistically open fires mean you get nicely grilled if you're located near them and you freeze to death if you're across the other side of the room.

The other form of heating that can be problematic is any kind of hot air device. Although they are very powerful and heat a large area up very quickly, they are also very noisy. I remember a wedding I went to once – it was in November and the reception was in a marquee (bad idea – see below). While we were having dinner the place was cosy enough but when it came to the speeches, of course, no one could hear what the bridal party was saying despite their use of microphones. So the heaters were turned off. And although the speeches were excellent, by the end of the best man's very funny piece all the guests were turning various shades of blue.

Patio heaters are popular nowadays and do work somewhat better to warm marquee interiors or those of the temporary rigid structures sometimes used for receptions and banquets. If you're going for this type of reception, patio heaters are a reasonably effective – if rather energy-wasteful – option.

Marquees

This is where I go into chainsaw-murderer mode and rant about the use of marquees in, frankly, any weather and at any time of the year. As I said in Chapter 1, much as they offer relatively instant and relatively cheap accommodation for numerous guests, they are hot and sweaty in summer and bitterly cold at any other time. And because it is impossible to insulate marquees – even if they do come with a thick lining and a floor – you will be battling to keep the chills away, as I suggest above.

Also mentioned above is a type of temporary rigid structure which is a popular choice for businesses that organize corporate entertaining, company Christmas celebrations, etc. These are marginally more weatherproof than marquees but still, because they're essentially rather flimsy, they are difficult to keep properly warm – especially for guests who have the misfortune to sit near the walls.

In your shoes I would avoid either a marquee or its rigid cousin and instead choose a nice, solid building in which you know you and your guests will be comfortable, whatever the weather outside.

Light – or lack thereof

Certainly in the darker half of the year and probably for all but the months of May, June and July in the UK and northern Europe, by the time your wedding celebrations are over it will be very dark outside. Particularly when the weather is bad and the ground may be wet and slippery, it's essential that there is good lighting outside the reception venue and all the way to the car park.

Bear in mind that some guests may be less than sober when they leave the reception. If you combine that with a slushy or muddy footpath in very dim light, it's a recipe for disaster at worst and some dirty clothes and bruised egos at best.

If you are using minibuses to ferry guests from reception to car park (or their overnight accommodation) ensure that the drivers have strong torches (flashlights) they can use to help guests through any dimly lit areas.

Seasonal considerations

Although it can be a lovely idea to plan your wedding to happen very close to Christmas, New Year's or Valentine's Day, bear in mind that these are extremely busy times of the year for most commercial venues. So not only is it harder to get the day and time you want, but also you'll be paying a lot more for it than you would at an off peak time.

Also bear in mind that many such venues will have their own seasonal decorations in place already and probably won't take kindly if you and your team show up and change everything around for the wedding reception.

It's well worth establishing that issue well in advance so that there are no misunderstandings nearer the time. However, with careful and tactful negotiation, you could find you save quite a lot on the cost of decorations by planning your wedding to be themed and timed for these occasions and cashing in on the decorations already placed — and paid for — by the venue itself.

Another season consideration is the fact that a potentially significant number of your guests may want overnight accommodation when they attend your wedding — whereas should you have got married in the summer they may have decided to venture home afterwards.

If you want to schedule your wedding around the critical Christmas, New Year or (to perhaps a slightly lesser extent) Valentine's Day, be sure to allow enough time to be successful in booking adequate rooms for the guests who don't want to risk travelling home in potentially bad weather conditions.

More decoration thoughts

Some of the autumn, winter and spring themes (see Chapter 3), though exciting and imaginative and all that, do actually involving some fairly heavy 'set dressing' in whatever venue you choose for your reception (and ceremony, if it's to be held there). Particularly when you start talking in terms of bagpipe players, ice sculptures, fake snow on the windows and elsewhere, and so-on, you might find the management of the venue less than enthusiastic ... they'll be thinking about potential disruption to other venue users, hotel guests trying to get some sleep, muck and mess that will take days to clean up (trust me, fake snow can be a doozer to get off), ice sculptures thawing and drenching the carpets, etc.

Before you firm up on any plans and themes, whether wild or not, be sure you and the venue management are in total agreement as to what you can and can't do, and get that agreement in writing.

Ceremony and reception in the same venue

In fairness the point I'm about to make can apply to summer weddings as well, but it becomes more relevant the colder and wetter the weather is outside.

My good friend Leanne got married in March a couple of years ago, at the Mappin Pavilion at London Zoo — a gorgeous venue, licensed for civil weddings, and equally superb for a dinner dance afterwards. However, it took the venue management quite some time to reconfigure the seating and arrangements from those for the ceremony, to those for the dinner dance.

Not to worry, thought the bridal couple. Guests will love the opportunity to look around the zoo and appreciate the animals. What they didn't take into consideration was not really the fact that weather conditions were likely to be cool; that, they did think about.

What some of their guests failed to think about was that simple but crucial matter of a gap between ceremony and reception — whereby despite the warm attention of the zoo animals, they might find themselves getting a bit chilly in their smart wedding clothes — should have prompted them bringing stout coats and other warm garments. March in London can be very, very cold, and it was.

Yet nothing could be done to speed up the process of converting the venue for the reception.

The moral to this story? If your autumn, winter or spring wedding venue requires converting from that of ceremony to that of reception, for Heaven's sake make sure your guests have somewhere to go that's warm, dry and comfortable. (And if the venue is a zoo, make sure guests know to bring warm coats and shoes for the interim period.)

Photogenic environs please

I have droned at some length about the need for suitable indoor locations for your wedding photographs and video in Chapter 7, but it's worth picking up on that here too if only briefly.

Considering the fact that your outdoor options for photographs and video footage at your reception venue are going to be limited in the cooler, darker months, when choosing a venue for a wedding during these times you need to be considerably more aware of its photogenic opportunities than if you were getting married in the summer.

Also, bearing in mind that whatever photo opportunities available at the place of your ceremony may be limited due to low light or other circumstances, the opportunities available at your reception venue may become even more important that they might have been otherwise.

6 Arranging food and drinks

With the vast range of foods available in the UK these days, there's virtually no need for your wedding feast to be restricted in any way. Whatever exotic dish takes your fancy is, in theory at least, available — at a price.

I haven't included any recipes in this book because I sincerely hope you brides aren't planning to do your own catering! However, I have made a number of suggestions and should whoever is doing your catering not know how to prepare one of these dishes, the recipes are easily found on the internet via your favourite search engine. Failing that, get in touch with me and I'll put you on to the right track (suze@suzanstmaur.com).

As some of you might already know my last book about weddings is, *How To Get Married In Green* — which is all about eco-friendly weddings. In there I go into some detail about enjoying foods that are (a) locally produced and (b) in season at the time of your wedding. And although here, strictly speaking, we're not talking about keeping your wedding 'green' to any great extent, seasonal foods do offer a huge bonus to whoever wants to eat them; not only is there the 'green' element to consider, but also, they taste fantastic.

So let's have a look at what foods may be the most appropriate for the cooler-months wedding.

Foods in season

October

In the UK, this is peak harvest time and you can benefit from the ultra colour-ful range of veggies like pumpkins, squashes and so-on. Elderberries are on the list for harvesting, too, and although they may not have so many culinary uses apart from those involved with elderberry jelly, they can be turned into some sensational wine — something you may want to consider if you're going for an organic/local produce menu.

Other features of October include UK-produced autumn lamb, which has a stronger flavour than spring lamb, although it is equally delicious. At this time of the year though, go for lamb dishes that involve some long, slow cooking, like lamb shanks, rather than the recipes for spring lamb which tend to focus on the fact that lamb from that seasons tends to be lighter, more tender, but lacking in such quite strong flavour.

If you're into game, grouse is still in season now despite having been in the menu since the 'glorious 12th' of August, and can be an interesting and tasty main course for a sit-down dinner reception. And if you're into slightly more exotic birds, guinea fowl are in season now too. Often people are rude about guinea fowl, saying they are just a skinnier version of chicken to be served at banquets, dinners and wedding receptions, but don't rule them out. Properly cooked and accessorized, they can be delicious, and regardless of some people's cynicism they do taste more interesting than, and different from, chicken.

Other types of game are coming into season by now, too, so check them out if this is something you fancy on your menu.

Now, if you love oysters, bear in mind that they are available at this time. Speaking as someone who has a violent shellfish allergy I would strongly advise you to offer a non-shellfish alternative if you want oysters at your wedding, but at the end of the day, it's your party and you must have what you love!

November

You may be forgiven for thinking that November is a no-no month for just about everything in the UK, but happily that's just not true.

Root vegetables like parsnips really come into their own now as do chestnuts and beetroot, plus things like cabbage and swede, not to mention potatoes, fruits like cranberries and quinces (yum for making jelly) and still, the inevitable pumpkins.

As for meat, goose is in full season now — despite being a fatty bird to roast its meat is quite delicious and would make a tasty choice for non-vegetarians at your wedding dinner. Vegetarians can dine glamorously on dishes involving seasonal veg, which are still in abundance.

December

If your wedding is in late December, particularly, you may want to take advantage of the classic, traditional Christmas menus available at this time of year. However, bearing in mind that in the UK, at least, many of us will be eating at least one Christmas dinner anyway — if not more, if we go to business or company Christmas lunches — you may prefer to choose something entirely different for your wedding menu. Much as the shops will all be full of turkeys, Christmas puddings and mince pies, there are a number of alternatives in season at this time.

Wild duck is available now and usually is far more tasty than the cultivated variety — less fatty, too. Goose is still in season and is something a little out of the ordinary, although ironically a few generations ago goose was more of a traditional choice than turkey. If you prefer fish, or want to incorporate a fish course in your wedding menu, sea bass is at its best now and it can be prepared in a large number of different ways.

Vegetables are plentiful and include beetroot, sprouts, red cabbage, celeriac, white celery, turnips, parsnips and swede — and most of those are perfect in a vegetarian roast vegetable dish, as well as being lovely accompaniments to meat or fish.

January

For main course choices we still have turkey, goose, duck and guinea fowl in relative abundance but now they are joined by some delicious fishy options like scallops and lobster. As I mentioned above, do be careful of offering a shellfish dish in your wedding menu; some people (like me!) have violent allergies to shellfish and can't eat it for that reason. Also remember that many people do not eat shellfish (or pork) for religious reasons.

Vegetables in season are still in relatively good supply, including most of the root vegetables plus squash and early leeks. Pears are around for consideration as dessert options, and forced rhubarb is beginning to make an appearance now, too.

February

February's choices are very similar to those of January, with the addition of some further fishy treats like mussels and halibut. In addition to the range of fruit and veg mentioned under the January heading, you'll also see the emergence of chicory and cabbage — both tasty ingredients that make a lovely winter salad.

You can also cook chicory, although it's not done so much in the UK — this is a dish handed down to me by my Belgian relatives. You simply braise the chicory very gently in a generous blob of butter, some salt and pepper and a splash of water until it's soft and semi-opaque. Chopped chicory also makes a good stir-fry ingredient. Delicious ... however, I digress and must remember this is not a recipe book.

March and into April

Once again, we're looking at a similar line-up of in-season foods as we were in January and February, but now we're beginning to see the arrival of early fresh green and other vegetables. These include parsley, mint, purple sprouting broccoli, sorrel and leeks. The early rhubarb is coming along well now. Once we nudge into April we begin to see some early spinach which is delicious gently sweated with some sorrel.

This is the time to get some wonderfully tender and delicate spring lamb, of course, perhaps roasted or pan fried with a sprinkling of rosemary. Rosemary is in flower at this time of year, and the small blue blooms are not only entirely edible but also look very pretty in salads or even as a garnish in a dessert dish.

Fresh morel mushrooms are at their best now and make a very useful ingredient for both meat and vegetarian dishes. And by early April we're starting to see some European strawberries which somehow seem to have more flavour than those from further away.

Food and drinks to match wedding themes

Key events and holidays nearly always have at least part of the celebrations involving food and drink, and even if the rest of your wedding is not necessarily themed around such an event you may want to consider the menus available in any case (most of them are delicious). In this section I have described a number of these events but the list is by no means complete — especially where religious occasions are concerned. Still, I hope what I have included gives you some 'food for thought' (sorry!).

So, in roughly chronological order then ...

Canadian Thanksgiving (2nd Monday in October)

Canadian Thanksgiving takes place on the second Monday of October, making it some six-and-a-bit weeks earlier than the US version. Essentially, the traditional food eaten for both Canadian and US versions is similar, but there are a few subtle differences.

Key elements of a Thanksgiving dinner are:

- Roast turkey
- Stuffing
- Mashed potatoes
- Gravy
- Cranberry sauce
- Various vegetable dishes
- Pumpkin pie

Although the roast turkey tends to be done in a straightforward manner, some families now deep fry the bird. This is quite an involved process as you can imagine, having to dunk a ten kilo or more turkey in a vat of boiling oil, but the result is very good, tender meat and the cooking time is a fraction of that taken in a conventional oven. Anyway, that's probably not something you want to suggest to your UK wedding caterers!

North American stuffing (called 'dressing' there) tends to be lighter than our UK stuffing. Although some recipes do include sausage meat, preferred ingredients tend to be wild rice, mushrooms, fruits, raisins, onions and chestnuts.

Where the North Americans do splash out is on fancy vegetable dishes; there's none of our staunch British plain boiling or steaming for them. You'll find carrots or squash glazed with maple syrup, green beans often served with butter and flaked almonds or chopped walnuts, turnips or sweet potato mashed with cream and spices, etc. There are more of these and other exotic Thanksgiving specialities under 'US Thanksgiving' below.

Halloween (31 October)

I can see my editor's eyebrows rise in alarm even as I type this, but you might well want to consider a Halloween theme for a small-to-medium late October wedding and if so, here are some ideas for your menu.

Obviously pumpkins are an essential part of Halloween and, when you don't cut them out as jack o'lanterns, can be cooked and served in a surprisingly large range of dishes. With pumpkins being in season and available in plentiful quantities at this time, you may want to consider some of these dishes, especially as vegetarian options, even without recourse to other Halloween themeing and décor.

So, in savoury dishes you can have:

- A huge variety of different pumpkin-based soups
- Pumpkin ravioli, lasagne, risotto or pancakes
- Roasted, grilled, stewed, au gratin ...
- Stir-fried with other vegetables
- As a Thai curry, with chilli, or as an Indian-style curry with fish or shellfish
- Mashed and creamed alone or with other vegetables

Plus there's the choice you might expect of dessert dishes: pumpkin bread, pie, cheesecake, ordinary cake, scones and muffins.

If you do decide to go for a Halloween theme, don't forget to include some of the other traditional foods like toffee apples, other, colourful fruit, sweets and candied fruits, popcorn, corn-on-the-cob, etc.

Bonfire Night (5 November)

If you decide to combine your wedding celebrations with some fireworks around early November, you might like to theme the food accordingly, especially if your reception is to be informal and relatively small. Some foods you could consider, then, are:

Hearty, warming soups

Roasted chestnuts

Jacket (baked) potatoes with various fillings

Grilled or barbecued sausages, hot dogs (frankfurters), chops, chicken joints, burgers

Chilli con carne

Cassoulet

Bread rolls

Roasted vegetables

Fried onions

Corn-on-the-cob

Garlic bread

Toasted marshmallows

Baked apples with cream or custard

Bananas baked either in the over or on the bonfire, in their skins and wrapped in foil

Apple pie

Drinks, of course, should consist of the warming variety, whether alcoholic or not. Various recipes are available for hot punches, spiced hot cider, mulled wine, plus of course tasty hot chocolate for non-drinkers and hot chocolate with a drop of rum or whisky for those who don't mind a tipple.

Diwali (October or November)

Not being Indian/Hindu and never having been there, I'm sad to say, I can only relay to you what I have researched about Diwali which is also known as the Festival of Light.

One thing that my research as revealed is the extraordinary range of delicious food prepared to help celebrate this festival; in fact for many, Diwali involves a huge feast which takes several days to prepare. The dishes, obviously, are very Indian in nature but as we in the UK tend to love Indian food whether we are Asian or not, a wedding feast taking place at around the time of Diwali could well appeal to everyone in its culinary delights.

The range of Diwali dishes is as wide and varied as the very culture of Hindu India itself, ranging from a huge selection of sweet, spicey dishes to numerous, largely vegetarian curries and other savoury dishes. The days of Diwali and New Year are days when families feast together and whether you are Hindu or not, some of the relevant recipes would make the most wonderful contributions to UK winter wedding menus.

Bear in mind that should you want to consider a Diwali menu, many Indian restaurants in the UK are likely to offer these should you decide to hold your wedding reception at their premises, and some will also be willing to provide the food on an outside catering basis.

Should your caterers want to check out Diwali recipes, a quick entry into your favourite search engine as '***diwali+recipes***' will provide a multitude of tasty options.

US Thanksgiving (4th Thursday in November)

To a certain extent I have gone into North American Thanksgiving earlier on in the chapter in relation to the Canadian version which not only comes before 'US' alphabetically, but also comes first in my estimation, but that's only because I'm a Canadian born and bred! However, in all fairness US Thanksgiving is the fourth Thursday of November, so its inclusion here in my roughly chronological listing is not inappropriate.

Obviously the turkey dinner in these circumstances is key to the whole proce-dure, and in fact our own UK use of turkey as a celebration centerpiece – not for Thanksgiving which we don't do here, but for Christmas – comes directly from North America and its British founding fathers. This is despite the fact that wild turkeys apparently have been around for ten million years or so, although not in the British Isles as far as we know.

It is said that turkeys were first introduced into Britain by a British trans-Atlantic trader who managed to get a few live birds over here from North America in about the 16th century. Although it's said that King Henry VIII enjoyed dining on turkey, it wasn't until King Edward VII started scoffing turkey for Christmas dinner that this bird became popular over here.

Anyway, we're not talking Christmas now, but Thanksgiving. As I have given you the basics of North American Thanksgiving in the Canadian bit, let me now share some additional Thanksgiving dishes you might like to get your caterers to consider – despite the fact that some of these go back over many years.

Some typical US Thanksgiving menus in the 17th century might have included:

- Wild turkey
- Venison
- Stuffing made from herbs, stuffing, oats
- Seasonal wild fowl
- Wild corns
- Seafood like lobsters, eels, mussels, oysters
- Grapes, white and red, and very sweet and strong also. Strawberries, gooseberries, raspberries, etc. Plums of the various tree sorts, with black and red being almost as good as a damson; abundance of roses, white, red, and damask; single, but very sweet indeed.

OK, now let's move on to the 19th century. What were the US Thanksgiving culinary treasures then – and can we resurrect those for winter wedding menus here in the UK now? I suspect the answer is, overall, yes – especially as recipes for such delights are available on the internet.

Here are some of the Thanksgiving dishes you might have encountered in 19th century USA:

- Oxtail soup
- Oyster soup
- Cod with egg sauce
- Lobster salad
- Roast turkey, stuffed
- Roast goose
- Pigeon
- Quail
- Woodcock
- Bass (fish)
- Stuffed chicken with pork
- Chicken pie
- Boiled ham
- Pressed beef
- Boiled tongue
- Potatoes
- Turnip sauce
- Chestnuts, various dishes
- Squash
- Onions
- Gravy sauce
- Cranberry sauce
- Apple and cranberry sauce
- Oyster sauce
- Mixed pickles

- Cold slaw
- Browned mashed potatoes
- Boiled onions
- Corn (sweetcorn)
- Sweet potatoes
- Roasted broccoli
- Pumpkin pie and other pumpkin desserts
- Plum and plain pudding, with sweet sauce
- Mince, pumpkin and apple pies
- Orange ice
- Cheese

Now, moving on into the 20th century, it would appear that the US obsession with oysters had not diminished to any great extent. Here are some typical dishes from some early 20th century American Thanksgiving menus:

- Oysters (raw, on half shell)
- Oysters with Sherry
- Oyster bisque or other soup
- Clam chowder
- Consomme
- Sheepshead
- Mutton dish or broth
- Roast turkey with oyster sauce
- Roast turkey stuffed with oysters
- Various game bird options (depending on where in US)
- Roast capon
- Fried oysters
- Oyster stew

- Poultry pie with cauliflower
- Scalloped oysters (again?)
- Cranberry sauce, preserve, jelly etc
- Croquette potatoes
- Various lettuce-based salads
- Various stuffings including chestnut, etc. (see 'Canadian Thanksgiving' above; recipes haven't changed much in the last 150 years ...)
- Cheese and biscuits
- Pumpkin pie (of course)
- Pecan pie

And as for the 21st century? Well, I could say that anything goes, but knowing the North Americans as I do (after all, I am one) I think it might be a while before they deviate much from their traditional Thanksgiving Day menus. My own view is that apart from perhaps adding some more vegetarian options which would bring their bills of fare up to date, they've got it pretty much right. Bon appétit.

St Andrew's Day (30 November) (Scotland)

You don't have to be Scottish to enjoy Scottish food, and as in the UK there isn't a lot going on at the end of November other than the crazy commercial rat race in the run-up to Christmas, you may well like to choose St Andrew's Day as a theme. A quick search via your favourite search engine will reveal a number of Scottish delicacies in recipe format, but for the moment here are some ideas.

Soups and starters

- Scotch broth
- Scottish cullen skink
- Cock-a-leekie
- Tattie soup

- Lentil soup
- Abroath toasties
- Seafood in whisky cream
- Prawns in whisky

Main course

- Fresh salmon
- Salted herring
- Smoked salmon
- Kedgeree
- Finnan Haddie
- Beef in whisky sauce
- Aberdeen Angus steak
- Chicken in Drambuie
- Lamb chops with Dundee marmalade
- Stovies
- Roast grouse (season ends mid-December, but there are frozen options!)
- Scotch eggs
- Haggis
- Vegetarian haggis
- White pudding

Desserts and sweets

- Crannachan
- Scottish Clootie Dumpling
- Shortbread
- Dundee cake

- Angus toffee
- Scottish tablet
- Oranges in Drambuie
- Caledonian cream

Drinks

- Whisky of all kinds!
- Whisky Hot Toddy (great on a cold day)
- Numerous whisky-based and Drambuie-based cocktails
- Drambuie
- Glayva
- Rusty Nail
- Gaelic coffee

Hanukah (December)

There are numerous traditional dishes associated with this Jewish holiday and whether you pick dishes from here for religious reasons or not, most of them are truly delicious. (I could eat latkes until the cows come home.) So here are a few ideas to get you started.

Starters

- Pickled herring
- Chopped liver
- Vegetable latkes
- Potato latkes
- Blintzes
- Gefilte fish
- Chicken soup

Main courses

- Duck with honey
- Baby chicken with honey
- Boiled chicken
- Fried chicken
- Apricot chicken
- Beef and fruit casserole
- Beef brisket
- Lamb with honey glaze
- Vegetarian chilli

Desserts and sweets

- Hanukah cookies (various)
- Apple dumplings
- Rugelach
- Rice pudding
- Suphganiot
- Sweet potato latkes

Christmas (25, 26 December)

Many people getting married in the second half of December would sooner poke themselves in the eye with a sharp stick than have 'Christmas fare' for their wedding meal. However, there are those of us who want to go with the flow, and take advantage of the festive décor and ambience that's already up and running (and partly, in some venues at least, paid for by someone else). And quite apart from that rather cynical consideration, some of us just love roast turkey and all the trimmings.

Let's recap, then, on just what the traditional UK Christmas menu looks like.

- Light starter like smoked salmon, parma ham and melon, prawn cocktail, salad

- Roast turkey

- Stuffing made from sausage meat, herbs, dried apricots, breadcrumbs, onion, etc

- Chestnut stuffing

- Chipolata sausages

- Roast cocktail sausages wrapped in streaky bacon

- Bread sauce

- Cranberry sauce

- Gravy

- Roast potatoes

- Selection of various vegetables

- Christmas pudding flambéed with brandy

- Sweet dessert sauce

- Custard

- Cream

- Brandy or rum butter

However, in addition to or instead of the current traditional Christmas fare, let's take a look at some ideas that, despite being a bit different (and some are really 'off the wall') could make some fascinating choices for an unique Christmas wedding menu. Recipes for all these suggestions can be found on the internet via your favourite search engine.

Victorian Christmas dishes

- Clear turtle soup

- Oysters

- Christmas pie (including various fowl and game meat)

- Mincemeat (made with both fruits and real meat)

- Mincemeat pudding
- Rabbit and hare pie
- Herring pie
- Mince pies (with fruit and mutton)
- Mince pies (with lemon, fruit, and lots of booze)
- Roast goose (still popular now as an alternative to turkey)
- Roast rib of beef with Yorkshire pudding (particularly popular in northern England)
- Boar's head (okay, perhaps not!)
- Sugar plums
- Spotted Dick
- Plum pudding

Non-British Christmas dishes

- Cheese fondue (France)
- Baked sturgeon (Russia — you could use other fish!)
- Beef cassoulet (France)
- Meat and potato casserole (Greece)
- Meat balls (Sweden)
- Champagne risotto (Italy)
- Roast shoulder of lamb with saffron (Spain)
- Roast lamb with potatoes (Greece)
- Roast pheasant or guinea fowl (Italy)
- Roast pork (Argentina)
- Veal with quince (Greece)
- Andalusian rice salad (Spain)
- Buche de Noel (dessert — France)
- Christmas nut roll (Hungary)

- Chocolate caliente (Mexico)
- St Nicholas cake (Russia)
- Baklava (Greece)
- Kataifi (Greece)
- Panatone (Italy)

New Year/Hogmany (31 December – 2 January)

As we all know only too well Scotland is the place to look to for New Year celebrations that rival those celebrated in other countries, and the choice of a Hogmany menu can be delightful – especially if everyone has spent the previous week or so stuffing themselves on southern, Christmas fare.

For Scottish menu suggestions, please look back at the section I put together on St Andrew's Day, as your food and drink options are very similar here. However, I do feel that despite the Scots' fondness for whisky, some champagne or other fizzy equivalent for your speeches – and for midnight – are entirely excusable even if the rest of your reception is entirely Scottish-themed.

Just out of interest, there are a few menu ideas the Scots use on their very busy New Year's celebrations which go on for not one, but two days. With all the drinking and 'first-footing' they need (a) sustenance to help people mop up the celebratory whisky and (b) want dishes that can be left, heated up if necessary and consumed on the run.

Here, therefore, are some potentially useful recipe ideas you might like to incorporate into your wedding menu, especially if it's going to be a buffet.

- Scotch pancakes, either savoury (with smoked salmon) or sweet
- Various Scottish soups
- Lamb stew with black pudding
- Pheasant casserole
- Kedgeree
- Chicken casserole with whisky and apple

- Venison collops
- Peaches in whisky

Burns' Night (25 January)

Once again, we're in Scotland! However Burns' night is just the most wonderfully romantic celebration and, unlike St Andrew's Day and Hogmany, does tend to have a particularly specific menu. So here it is.

To begin, a soup — probably Cock-a-leekie. There are loads of recipes for this and other soups available on the internet and accessible via your favourite search engine.

Next we have the main course and here is where we become pretty restricted in our choices.

- Haggis
- Tatties
- Neaps
- Whisky
- ...!!

As you know the entry of the haggis into the dining room on Burns' night is an incredibly ceremonious occasion (especially if the participants are virulently Scottish and have had a few snifters) and should you decide upon this option for your wedding feast you will undoubtedly be comfortable with the accompanying pipe music and recitations of Rabbie Burns' various œuvres. For details on this, see Chapter 3.

Now, there are some people who will stick their noses up at the culinary standards of a typical Burns supper. However, I have experienced Burns' nights in Scotland where the menu began with a choice between seafood or smoked salmon, followed by a course consisting of a couple of small slices of haggis, an ice-cream scoop of ridiculously creamy mashed 'tatties' along with an equally ridiculously creamy scoop of 'neaps' (turnip to the uninitiated) accompanied by a small tumbler full of malt whisky strong enough to dissolve your tonsils, assuming you still have some. That was then followed by a main course of Aberdeen Angus beef so tender that it melted in your mouth. The desserts were equally gorgeous. And I would defy anyone to say that a meal like that is anything but utterly comparable to *haute cuisine* anywhere else in the world.

Valentine's Day (14 February)

Where food is concerned, Valentine's Day tends to focus on aphrodisiac stuff that will further enhance already burgeoning emotions.

The origins of so-called aphrodisiac foods are a little blurry to put it mildly, and their efficacy is even more blurry. However, in our modern world we're told that these are 'must-haves' on a Valentine's menu. Whether you want to take this advice further into your wedding menu is up to you, especially considering that it may create aphrodisiac effects on people for whom it's not necessarily appropriate. However many of the following ingredients, whether 'aphrodisiac' or not, go towards compiling some delicious dishes that will really enhance your wedding menu.

Starters

- Avocados
- Oysters
- Asparagus
- Caviar
- Truffles

Main courses

- Anything (meat-based or vegetarian) prepared with one or more ingredients from the miscellaneous list below

Desserts

- Pretty well anything connected with chocolate. How about a chocolate fountain?

- Raspberries
- Strawberries
- Pineapple
- Bananas
- Figs

Miscellaneous

- Cardamon
- Aniseed
- Basil
- Cinnamon
- Garlic (yes, smelly breath or not)
- Nutmeg
- Ginger
- Mustard
- Honey
- Vanilla
- Pine nuts
- Almonds
- Carrots
- Chillis

St David's Day (1 March) (Wales)

To most people, Welsh food is flagged up by the noble leek and indeed leeks do form a significant part of St David's Day celebration meals. However as you would expect there is a great deal more to Welsh food than that. Here are a few ideas to get you started; the internet and your favourite search engine will reveal many tasty Welsh recipes you can select.

Starters

- Salads using Caerphilly and other Welsh cheeses
- Cawl Cennin (leek soup)
- Cawl Lafwr (soup with seaweed)
- Mousse with leeks
- Welsh goat's cheese and leek tart
- Welsh cheese pudding
- Cockle cakes
- Laver bread

Main courses

- Monkfish with Laverbread
- Cod pie
- Cockle pie
- Herrings stuffed with walnuts
- Rabbit and lentil casserole
- Welsh lamb with honey
- Spring lamb pie
- Pembroke lamb pie
- Welsh trout with bacon and chives
- Welsh fish stew
- Breast of lamb bake
- Lamb stew with leeks and pearl barley (lovely idea for a cold winter's day)
- Salt duck
- Vegetarian main course options

Desserts etc

- Apple pastry

- Rice pudding the Welsh way

- Bread pudding from Monmouth

- Lemon meringue dessert

- Hot butter sponge

- Bakestone cakes

- Various delicious Welsh cheeses

St Patrick's Day (17 March) (Ireland)

St Patrick's Day brings a number of emotions to mind here in the UK and should you have Irish connections, or not — but wish to partake of Irish traditions plus food and drink — on your wedding day, here are some notions to get you thinking along appropriate lines. Needless to say your trusty internet via a favourite search engine will reveal far more gastronomic ideas, as indeed will various cook books you can buy in the shops.

However, here are some thoughts to get you in the mood.

Starters

- Irish potato soup

- Pancakes with black pudding and bacon

- Baked scallops

Main courses

- Baked scallops

- Irish salmon

- Irish lamb (various)

- Irish stew

- Beef in stout

- Beef in stout with oysters
- Vegetarian main course options
- Potato cakes (e.g. Boxty)
- Colcannon
- Champ

Desserts

- Cheesecake with Irish whisky cream
- Irish cream liqueur dessert
- Chocolate pie with Bailey's
- Frozen Irish liqueur dessert
- Whiskey pie
- Potato pie (sweet – yes, really!)

Drinks

- Guinness
- Irish whisky
- Bailey's

Easter (March or April)

Needless to say there are numerous traditional tasties associated with Easter, but here I only have room to remind you of a few. There are hundreds if not thousands more and your caterer should be able to come up with some delightful Easter ideas for your menu – and if you want to give him or her some further ideas key '***Easter recipes***' into the search box of your favourite search engine.

Starters

- Easter eggs (savoury)
- Seasonal spring salad
- Seasonal soup options

Main courses

- Good Friday fish pie
- Easter lamb – various (i.e. hundreds of) recipes and treatments
- Roast or boiled ham
- Turkey or goose (yes, they're becoming more popular Easter choices in the UK)
- Vegetarian options
- Seasonal side dish options

Desserts

- Hot cross buns with various fillings and icings
- Easter eggs (sweet, various)
- Various cakes and sweets
- Simnel cake

St George's Day (23 April) (England)

As I said in Chapter 3, St George's Day has rather less in the way of cultural 'must-haves', so as long as you what you do – and eat – is 'English', you can't really go wrong. Medieval, Elizabethan and Victorian themed menus are options, but I thought it might be fun to resurrect some menu ideas from 'typical English food' served in restaurants around the middle of the 20th century. Some of these dishes are still current, of course, but others have been almost forgotten – undeservedly – due to our modern focus on food from other cultures.

Starters

- Chestnut soup with apples
- Melba toast and butter
- Smoked salmon
- Salmon mousse with cucumber
- Salmon, trout, or other fish paté

- Liver paté with toast
- Walnut paté with Stilton
- Egg mayonnaise
- Prawn cocktail
- Potted shrimps
- Deep-fried whitebait
- Parma ham and melon
- Oxtail soup
- Minestrone soup
- Cream of (chicken, mushroom, asparagus) soup

Main courses

- Baked cod in parsley sauce
- Fish and chips
- Roast beef with Yorkshire pudding
- Roast pork with apple sauce
- Roast lamb with mint sauce
- Lancashire hotpot
- Baked ham with pineapple slices
- Beef and carrots, boiled
- Roast beef and Yorkshire pudding
- Beef Wellington
- Steak and kidney pie/pudding
- Roast lamb
- Shepherd's pie
- Cottage pie
- Coronation chicken

- Roast chicken
- Chicken a la King
- Roast Aylesbury duck with orange sauce
- Cornish pasties
- Bubble and squeak
- Roast potatoes
- Cauliflower cheese
- Grilled mushrooms

Desserts

- Bread and butter pudding
- Spotted dick
- Summer pudding
- Syllabub
- Treacle tart
- Sherry trifle
- Rice pudding
- Apple pie
- Rhubarb /apple/etc. crumble
- Gooseberry fool
- Lemon meringue pie
- Black Forest gateau

7 Photography and videography

Before we go any further, it's probably sensible to share a few thoughts about the basics of wedding photography for the benefit of those who choose to DIY. Now, please bear in mind that I am hopeless at the technology surrounding either still or moving pictures but, having worked as (a) a writer for both AV and video productions for many years, plus as (b) an art director of still photography and (c) a video director for almost as long, I do remember a few useful titbits that you can pass on to whoever does those all-important pix for your wedding.

Digital photography/videography

Being an old dinosaur of course I grew up with old-fashioned film-based still cameras as well as film motion pictures. However, not being *quite* that old, I got into the video age both when it was tape-based and then more recently digitally based.

And it's weird – speaking as that same old dinosaur I still can't credit the fact that you can now shoot, edit and produce the same standard of broadcast-quality video on a small camera and a laptop in a couple of days which in the 1980s, would have involved a crew of dozens in a project covering two or three weeks. Hey, that's what you get when you get old ... now. Never mind.

The *realpolitik* of digital photography/videography is that it works far better and more efficiently in varying light and other conditions, and basically allows you to shoot and enjoy a huge amount of material without going to the expense of having film processed. Beyond that of course it averts the need for the potentially polluting use of chemicals in its development, never mind all the use of resources required in creating prints, etc.

However, don't write off the simple film-based disposable stills camera altogether. In an emergency it can provide a cheap, quick and highly effective alternative when the fancier equipment goes wrong, encounters flat batteries, or experiences other technical glitches. Once you get home you can have your prints scanned so they can be used and viewed just as the digitally orig-inated versions can.

A few things to remember

Despite flash and other artificial lighting aids, as you might expect natural is best. Even when light conditions are less than perfect, encourage your photographer/videographer to use available light where possible; it looks better. Within reason, adjustments can be made on cameras to cope with quite a wide variety of light conditions.

The vast majority of amateur cameras and even some professional ones use built-in flash that is only effective across a few metres or so. Should your pho-tographer/videographer want to take longer shots than that, suggest that they use additional lighting — either separate flash or, if there is time and budget, (and in the case of video where flash is not an option) free-standing lights.

Another important point to consider is the shadows cast by flash or other harsh lighting. All good wedding photographers will know this, but if someone is DIYing — or you're using a local photographer in a far-flung location — make sure they do not stand you and the other figures too close to any walls, particularly if they are pale in colour. If this happens you get noticeable shad-ows falling in awkward places. Always stand as far out from a plain background as possible, as this will minimize the shadow problem.

Fussy backgrounds, too, can be a recipe for disaster. We've all heard stories about wedding pictures where there is a knight in armour peering over the groom's shoulder, or a deer's antler sticking out of the matron of honour's left ear. If you think this could be yet another urban myth, consider the following:

I got married on the 25th of October. It was pay day which was why hubby chose the date. All I recall is a mighty gale and standing outside the church watching inside-out umbrellas flying past. But to top it all we

> were so hard up we couldn't afford a photographer so as my ex husband works for the police we got our wedding photos done by a scene of crime officer. In every single one (taken indoors) I have a light fitting growing out of the back of my head.
>
> **R W.**

There's a moral here; do not make a police officer your first choice of wedding snapper, despite their undoubted expertise at photographing murder victims and burglary scenes. Also do not allow anyone to pose you and the rest of the bridal party in front of anything which might detract from the only important features of the day — you and your nearest and dearest.

Having said that, of course, it's worth remembering that a professional or keen amateur photographer or videographer can make good use of indoor features as props for your wedding pix. Ornamental fireplaces (not necessarily alight), sweeping staircases, minstrel galleries, plus of course church and other religious building interiors if permitted, can all make dramatic and effective backdrops — provided they remain as backdrops and do not intrude.

And if you're getting married in a particularly unusual location — the London Eye or Brighton Pier are examples — your photographer and videographer will need to be especially creative with the backdrops!

Cool climates in the northern hemisphere

If your wedding is to be in northern Europe during the autumn, winter or spring months you need to think carefully about any outdoor still or moving pictures, if only because there is a strong likelihood of cold and wet conditions making things difficult. If you are lucky enough to get a sunny day and the circumstances permit, the gentler, more flattering light cast by the sun when it's lower in the sky can make for some magical images — in fact much more interesting pictorially than when the sun is right above us.

By far the more pressing issue, however, is the cold and possibly wet conditions you may encounter and rather than risk your entire wedding party freezing to death despite woolly knickers, you might want to do yourselves a favour and forget outdoor shots.

But what outdoor shots could still be viable?

This is something you need to discuss with your wedding photographer/ videographer, but bear in mind how celebrities can be pictured looking stunning while emerging on to the red carpet at premieres, or how the paparazzi grab glamorous shots of them when they arrive/leave in their limousines. If you choose a reportage style for all or some of your wedding images, then even if it's raining or snowing when the bridal party arrives at the location or when the bride and groom leave for their honeymoon, much can be made of the 'in car' shots — whether formal or informal.

It's always a good idea to 'recce' the location of your ceremony and reception with the intended photographer some time before the date. Not only is this very helpful in organizing indoor posed shots, but also in working out where the sun — if out — will be at the time of your arrivals and departures and where outdoor shots might be feasible even if the weather is bad, with a little artificial help — e.g. a large church porch or awning over an hotel entrance.

Don't forget that in northern Europe although you might get bright sunshine when you arrive at your ceremony location in, say, the early afternoon, by the time you emerge an hour or so later it could be nearly dark.

Posed pictures

No matter how small and informal or large and grand your wedding, you will want to have at least a few formal, posed shots — certainly as still pictures, and possibly as part of your wedding video as well. As we've discussed already in this chapter counting on pretty posed pix in a glorious rose garden or on a neatly manicured lawn will probably be out of the question. However, as I've already suggested, don't rule out exterior shots altogether.

When I got married (this time!) it was in October in the UK but we had a really warm, balmy day and were able to get some lovely shots of us all grouped outside the very picturesque restaurant we had chosen for the celebratory lunch.

Similarly you can be lucky in northern Europe and get some warm, sunny days even in early spring.

The trick here, then, is to keep that option open and ensure you're prepared to take advantage of good outdoor conditions should they happen on the day. That means forewarning your photographer or videographer so they can visit the locations and pick places that would work weather permitting, and even considering details like packing a pair of flat shoes or boots in your wedding day kit bag — and suggesting the bridesmaids do the same.

Indoor posed pictures obviously require the same setting up whatever the time of year, although you probably won't be able to count on any natural daylight during our cooler months. One thing that applies particularly to weddings in the cooler months is the problem of what to do with guests while the pictures/formal footage are being shot. It's bad enough in summer to keep them hanging around outside the reception venue for half an hour, but in the winter it's asking for trouble. To avoid this problem it's best if you can arrange a separate room or area for the pictures to be done, while the non-participating guests are entertained elsewhere. See Chapter 5.

What else do you want to capture?

Often it's the small things that happen during a wedding that can make the day even more memorable, and it's a good idea to ensure someone is on watch to capture such little details on camera. Your professional photographer and/or videographer may well be able to do this, but especially if they have a hefty brief to get all the 'must-have' shots, there may not be sufficient time for them to look for the other things.

This is where friends who are handy with a camera can be very helpful, especially if you brief them well beforehand. Summer weddings probably offer more opportunities for these small gems, especially if the reception is held partly or totally out of doors, but indoor weddings still offer small gems of their own if you know where to look.

These include 'paparazzi' style shots of people mingling, chatting, laughing, whispering in each other's ears ... children getting mucky with cake on their faces, or crawling under the tables to make a 'den' ... elderly relatives catching up on gossip in a corner ... elderly relatives telling stories to small children ... bride, groom, or bridesmaid taking off her shoes and smiling with relief ... grandpa dancing with small grand-daughter ... mother of the bride showing off her jiving or tango skills ... and so on. Every wedding party is different and the key here is for whoever takes these pictures to know, or at least suspect beforehand, where the opportunities are going to arise so they are there ready to point and shoot. For that reason, you may get better results from pictures done by someone who knows you and your families/friends, rather than the professional photographer unless of course s/he is a personal contact as well.

Weddings in the snow

If you are in a snowy location like a ski resort, then many more options are open to you. Assuming it's daylight you may well be blessed with excellent, if rather reflective light, so make sure whoever is doing your pictures knows how to adjust the camera for the glare of snow-based shots — especially if the sun is shining at the same time. If the pictures are being taken outdoors after the sun has gone down your 'snapper' may well need to use a particular combination of lighting to achieve a good effect without making surrounding snow look dull and dirty.

My own view here is that if you are getting married in a snowy environment and want some good outdoor shots, use a local photographer/videographer who understands the intimacies of snow pictures. Well meaning amateurs can do a good job, of course, but if you're depending solely on an amateur 'snapper' do ensure they swat up on snow photography. And remember, digital cameras do their best but when trying to cope with huge contrasts between light and dark without some human assistance, they sometimes put their hands up and give up.

Weddings in tropical sunshine

In some ways taking either still or moving pictures in bright tropical or subtropical sunshine throws up similar problems as those in snowy conditions, especially with digital equipment. The more basic digital still and video cameras can sometimes struggle to cope with the harsh contrasts of light and dark and end up compromising by, say, featuring the dark colours and patterns of the groom's suit, leaving the bride's ivory work of art looking like a pale blob.

Obviously if you're using a professional or experienced amateur photographer or videographer then they will (a) know how to handle these strong contrasts pictorially and (b) their equipment will be sufficiently sophisticated to handle it well. But beware the DIYers, especially if they are the only ones capturing your wedding on film — well, on digital devices.

Another thing I've been warned about by several friends and acquaintances is that in many tropical and sub-tropical locations, darkness tends to fall surprisingly fast by comparison with the way it works in more temperate climates. So if you're getting married towards the early evening and want to take advantage of some stunning still pictures or footage of yourselves cantering along the beach at sunset, don't hang around expecting a lengthy twilight.

Obviously you will be able to find out the details of when it gets dark at your particular venue, but as a rough guide remember that the closer you get to the equator, the closer to 12 hours of darkness and daylight you get. It may sound stupid, but some people do assume that warm sunshine equals long days, as it does in northern latitudes. Further south, it doesn't.

8 Arranging honeymoons

To a certain extent you may well get some inspiration for honeymoon locations from Part 2, particularly in view of the fact that if you're getting married abroad you may well be combining that with a honeymoon in the same place.

Honeymoons that do not include the wedding ceremony or blessing usually are more straightforward to arrange – no more complex, really, than booking an ordinary holiday. However, there can be significant advantages if you let people know that you're going on honeymoon. Airlines might upgrade you to business or even first class. Hotels might upgrade you to a suite or even a bridal suite, and in any case are almost certain to provide some free flowers, fruit and maybe some champagne on your arrival.

Guiding advice here is do not be embarrassed or afraid to say this is a honeymoon when you book it – especially if you're going during an 'off peak' period as sometimes will be the case in our cooler months. Although there might be the unscrupulous one or two who think they could get away with hiking prices a bit considering it's your honeymoon, the vast majority will be more interested in the PR factor of helping you celebrate your marriage and will throw in the freebies.

Honeymoons in the UK

Unless you are particularly committed outdoor types, a honeymoon in a country cottage or by the sea are probably bad ideas during our cooler months. However, many people (*moi* included) love the thought of cuddling up in front of a roaring fire, sipping something delicious, dining on something even more delicious, then snuggling up under a duvet a metre thick in a four-poster bed in a charming country house hotel somewhere in the Shires.

I spent my second honeymoon (short though it was) at a wonderful such place called Chewton Glen (http://www.chewtonglen.com) in late October and despite the weather being foul outside, it was the most entrancing experience. And there are many more places like Chewton Glen around the UK; unlike Chewton Glen they are not all very expensive and tend to be even more romantic if the rain, wind, snow, hail etc. are creating hell outside the windows.

Some such venues are spas, as well, so you and your beloved can enjoy some pampering and cosseting in addition to lovely food and wine. Key '**country house hotels**' into your favourite search engine.

Of course you may not want anything as 'high-falutin' as a mini stately home with spa facilities and considering what such things can cost, I don't blame you. Such places do not seem to have seasonal downturns when we get to the October—March months and so prices tend not to take a downturn either.

Around the UK there are various smaller hotels and character pubs which offer accommodation. And provided that you pick the right place this can be just as romantic and delightful a venue as a 'posh' place costing hundreds more. Unlike the 'posher' places, these may well be dependent more on summer trade — especially if they are located in key summer tourist locations like the seaside, forests, parks and zoos, canals, rivers, etc. — so may well be keen to offer discounted prices during the autumn, winter and spring months. Assuming they're open, of course!

Places like these not only can offer comfortable accommodation, delicious food and attractive surroundings, but also the chance to mingle with the locals and have a social time if you choose to do so. And should the weather happen to be agreeable while you're there (after all it *does* happen sometimes, even in the UK during the cooler months) you have the added bonus of the chance to walk or cycle around some lovely surroundings as well as celebrating your nuptials indoors.

If you're really into UK-based activities have a look at what I've covered in Chapter 2, on hen and stag celebrations. That should give you some inspiration.

However, if you're like many couples getting married in the cooler months and wishing to honeymoon in the UK, you may well prefer to select a quiet, calm, comfortable, snugly, tasty option in one of our many delightfully characteristic venues. One good source of interesting locations and places to stay is Heritage magazine — a useful website to surf here is: http://www.heritagemagazine.co.uk.

And if you fancy something really unusual, have a look at: http://www.landmarktrust. org.uk. This organization offers about 180 buildings of historical interest ranging from stable blocks to cottages to follies to mausoleums which they have converted into comfortable accommodation. Most are available all year round.

Honeymoons a short way away

If you're not exactly feeling flush with money but want to experience a 'foreign' honeymoon during our cooler months, this is probably the best time for you to get a really worthwhile result within a short distance of the white cliffs of Dover.

To begin with, consider the *Channel Isles*. Deliberately I did not include them in Part 2 where I talk about foreign locations largely because the Channel Isles aren't really foreign — well, maybe, sort of — but at the end of the day they are strongly linked to the UK one way or another. I have only been briefly to Guernsey and not at all to the smaller islands, but Jersey I know well and can testify personally to its being a delightful place to visit even in the winter.

During the 'off peak' months Jersey sometimes hosts big business conferences and as I worked in that trade for a number of years, found myself in Jersey one February. The weather was milder than on the mainland and all the wonderful shops and restaurants were open — don't forget that Jersey offers significant tax advantages on shopping — and I'm sure it would be an ideal location for an out-of-season honeymoon. Hotel and other prices come down in our cooler months but the standards are equally high. If you like good shopping, unbelievably delicious food in glorious restaurants (they're only a short way from France, after all) and probably the best weather available within UK boundaries, give Jersey a look.

And further afield? Consider *northern France, Belgium and the Netherlands*. Easy and relatively cheap to get to. Weather that's similar to ours. But offering some interesting diversions not to mention superb food, excellent beer and wine, and some vibrant entertainment.

As you know, large cities do not close during the slow tourist seasons. That means that although the tourist trade has a way of dropping like a stone in cities/towns like *Brussels, Bruges, Amsterdam, Calais, Boulogne, Arras, Le Touquet*, etc., apart from some smaller businesses most things remain open from October until March or so. Naturally, prices fall. So provided you aren't averse to carrying an umbrella, consider very carefully the idea of honeymooning in these places. You'll get some amazing deals and benefit from their charm, cuisine and ambience while paying a fraction of summertime prices.

Honeymoons in 'warmer bits' of Europe

Personally, I can't really recommend going to places like the *south of France*, the coast of *Spain* (apart from the very southernmost bits), *Italy*, *Greece*, *Croatia* and other former *Yugo countries* plus even my beloved *Portuguese Algarve*, if you're not prepared to take a big chance on the weather from October to March. Unless, of course, you want to go for the ambience, culture, fun, food and booze without — necessarily — the sun, sand, sea etc!

Interestingly, whether it's global warming or what ... some friends of mine have just got back from a week in the Algarve in mid-May, having endured some pretty average and cool weather, whereas back in the UK we had temperatures 5–10°C higher than they did. Mind you, that's probably related to the crazy weather patterns we're dealing with currently. However, that does open up possibilities of experiencing good weather in such locations, no matter what the time of year.

Anyway, we need to look at this in perspective. If you want guaranteed sunshine and weather warm enough to sunbathe and swim, especially swim in the ocean, forget even southern Europe in the cooler months and instead save up for a trip to the Caribbean or Far East. However, if you're prepared to give and take over the weather in a southern Euro resort — maybe a few days of cloud and drizzle where you enjoy some shopping and delicious lunches and dinners under cover, followed by a day, two or three of glorious sunshine even in December or January — then head to such places.

As you can imagine, in the main they are in the very low season from a touristic point of view. Without doubt, many smaller hotels, restaurants, bars, etc. will be closed (a number of these owners head north for the season and run bars or restaurants in the Euro ski resorts) but provided that you choose larger towns, cities and resorts, you'll find the majority are still trading throughout the winter. And they will be delighted to see you and help you celebrate your honeymoon, as well as offering you some substantial discounts and other benefits due to your low-season booking.

City-based winter honeymoons

Although it is nice to wander around a city on foot admiring the sights and architecture, it's not essential — particularly if you're on honeymoon. Provided you don't mind shelling out for taxis or perhaps a rental car, even foul weather can be ignored to a large extent in an interesting city where there is lots to do under cover.

For example, *New York* — especially in the run-up to Christmas — is a wonderfully vibrant place even when the temperature is below freezing and the snow banks are piling up. You can participate in activities like outdoor ice skating and of course, shopping! That's in addition to the vast array of bars, bistros, restaurants, clubs, theatres and other entertainment which keeps going 365 days a year. The pre-Christmas period, as well as times like Christmas itself, New Year and Valentine's Day are likely to be pricier in terms of accommodation, but if you're on a tight budget it's nearly always possible to get decent accommodation at a good price in NYC whatever the time of year.

Other North American cities have fantastic winter carnivals which are beautiful to see and compensate for the cold with wonderful food and drinks — *Ottawa* and *Quebec City* are two that immediately spring to mind, but then of course I am Canadian! For more ideas key **'winter carnivals'+'north America'** into your favourite search engine.

Numerous European cities hold winter carnivals, too — especially in Germany where carnivals are very popular. However (and this is only personal opinion here) I think northern North American cities offer more in the way of winter activities either under cover, or else well-warmed by artificial means, because they are accustomed to long, cold winters and have built up their cities around that certainty.

Having said that, of course, provided you bundle up and carry your umbrellas, a winter honeymoon in cities like *Paris* or *Berlin* offers plenty of fascination both indoors and out. The further south you venture in Europe, the more you are likely to encounter wet rather than cold weather, but pack your winter woollies all the same. Much as they offer endless beauty to behold, delicious food and booze, lively entertainment and credit card-maxing shops to check out, cities like *Florence, Milan, Rome, Naples, Athens, Madrid, Barcelona, Lisbon* etc. can still be very chilly in the winter. Trust me — I have found that out the hard way. Autumn and spring months, though, can be delightful and much more comfortable for sight-seeing than in the hot summer months.

And don't forget some lovely cities closer to home. If you spend most of your time in rural or suburban surroundings, a winter honeymoon in the heart of *London, Edinburgh, Glasgow, York, Dublin* and various others can be just as much fun as a foreign version, plus will be cheaper (and possibly greener) than going further afield. London, especially, offers plenty to do under cover year round.

Honeymoons that are much further away

Once again, you can get a lot of relevant information in Part 2 of this book. However, as I mentioned above, a honeymoon in a far-flung location is going to be much cheaper and easier to organize than a wedding or wedding-honeymoon combination.

Particularly if you're on a tight budget, remember that this period is spring, summer and autumn in the southern hemisphere and also is the most popular time of the year for tourism in countries that hover nearer the equator. That means prices are likely to be at their highest in some places, and locations, hotels, etc. will be at their fullest.

One very useful piece of advice given to me by my good friend and PR consultant, Helen Moore, is to be wary of Christmas honeymoons. If you love all the traditional trimmings of a northern European Christmas you, like Helen, will find the rather silly attempts at Christmas decorations and menus made by some exotic, hot countries really unpleasant. I spent Christmas in Kenya one year and much though my hotel went to extreme efforts with the

Christmas lunch — turkey, carrots, Brussels sprouts all flown in at vast expense and cost to the environment — eating that on a terrace under parasols in 30°C heat just didn't do it for me.

If this sounds like you, you're better off spending Christmas in the UK and arranging your honeymoon either before or after. Or, if on the other hand, Christmas is not something you want to celebrate at all, choose a location such as Israel or Morocco where Christmas is not observed.

Part 2
Weddings abroad in our cooler months

Introduction

As our autumn, winter and spring months are a good time weather-wise to visit many foreign countries, I thought I should take a look at a variety of these destinations to see just what they offer at those times. Sadly I haven't room to include every country in the world — there are just shy of 200 altogether — so I have tried to pick those which will offer the most appeal to bridal couples.

As this is not a book about getting married abroad I haven't gone into the machinations of organizing a wedding outside the UK. There are some good books already in existence that cover this topic as well as many websites. And to find up-to-date information about the marriage regulations in the country of your choice, key '*getting married in* **(name of country)**' into your favourite search engine.

Please note that all the descriptions below are accurate as far as I can gather at the time of writing, and quite a lot of the information is my opinion based on what I've researched. These chapters are intended only to give you a flavour of each country's October to April options along with a very brief overview. So rather than take my word for it, do please research your choice of foreign country for your cooler-months wedding yourself if you don't know it well already, and very carefully too.

Local holidays and religious festivals

In general terms, it's worth remembering that in Christian countries and/or countries catering to tourists mainly from Western origins, the periods of Christmas, New Year and Easter are likely to be busy and more expensive. In predominantly Roman Catholic countries like France, Spain, Portugal and Italy, plus Greece (their Easter is later than the Roman Catholic or Protestant one), you may also find that these periods are impossible to book up for your wedding, as venues are either taken over by local people or are themselves closed for the festivities. If you want to arrange your wedding in countries where other religions are predominant, you need to check when their festivals and religious holidays are as if not you may run into similar issues.

If you're looking for a snow-covered wedding location then pick a winter wedding in Europe — countries such as Austria, Germany and the Czech Republic make wonderful winter snow destinations between November and March, especially if you choose a 'fairytale' castle location. Alternatively Canada can also provide more sure-fire snow and ice and has the spectacular Rocky Mountains in the west which make a fantastic backdrop to any wedding.

For those seeking sun, October to April are perfect months for a wedding in the southern hemisphere, South Africa, Australia and New Zealand offer diverse wedding locations during their spring and summer months, from a 'bush' wedding at a luxury lodge in South Africa to a city or countryside wedding in Australia, the summer months are popular for weddings. You're not guaranteed good weather but the chances are much higher than in Europe!

Flights to most places in the world cost less in winter as long as long as you avoid the expensive high spots during the Christmas, New Year and Easter holidays.

Steph
Marry Abroad
www.marryabroad.co.uk

The red tape factor

Although I haven't flagged them up individually, in this chapter I have included countries where you can get married legally, and also some where you can't (or whose marriages are not recognized legally in the UK) but where you can hold a blessing or other form of ceremony which you combine with a civil or religious marriage in the UK. There are some countries (like Spain and to a lesser extent, France) which do allow foreigners to get married but there is a long period of compulsory residence required for at least one partner, which can make it awkward. In this case it also may be that you need to consider a civil ceremony in the UK with a blessing in the country concerned.

The best plan is to contact the Embassy or High Commission of the country concerned and find out just what you can and can't do. Laws and regulations on these issues tend to change quite frequently, too, so you must ensure that your information is bang up to date.

Prices of flights to destinations around the world are often cheaper during these winter months as this is not the traditional summer holiday period. These months also happen to be summer in the Southern Hemisphere countries which really does open the options for couples – particularly if an outdoor theme is to play a part in the celebrations, the British weather is not known for its reliability even in summer so relocating your wedding to Southern Africa during their summer will almost guarantee good weather for your ceremony.

Special guests are more likely to be able to attend your wedding as it doesn't fall in the middle of their long-planned summer vacation. The couple is virtually in a perfect honeymoon location already so the overall cost of a wedding/honeymoon combination is reduced.

There are many more advantages but the key point is the amount of choice which a destination wedding will offer a couple. The world truly is your oyster!

Lauren
The Wedding Connection
www.TheWeddingConnection.info

Get expert help

Unless you are familiar with the country concerned, I would strongly recommend that you use the services of a specialized wedding planner for a foreign wedding in the autumn, winter and spring months. It's one thing organizing a wedding yourself in your local area where you know everyone and can keep a hands-on check on everything, but trying to do that in a foreign country with unfamiliar laws, culture, language, etc. – and that's hundreds or even thousands of miles away as well – is like stepping into a potential minefield. Several of the contributors to this book offer wedding planning services in a number of foreign countries; you'll find their details in Chapter 15, as well as comments from a few of them in this chapter. For countries not covered by my contributors, your search as described above will reveal specialist services for the country concerned.

Civil partnerships

If you're planning a civil partnership, at the time of writing (mid-2008) the UK recognizes these when they have taken place in the following countries:

- Belgium
- Canada
- Denmark
- Finland
- France
- Germany
- Iceland
- The Netherlands
- New Zealand
- Spain
- Sweden
- Switzerland
- USA, some states

Cruise ships

Before we look at the options on dry land, you might like to consider getting married on a cruise to somewhere like the Caribbean which is at its climatic best in our late autumn, winter and spring months. You'll need to check on the legalities of on-board wedding ceremonies. At the time of writing some ships do offer legal (civil) marriages whilst on the high seas, whereas others are restricted to ceremonies conducted while the ship is in port or within a short distance of it. A quick search using the phrase '*getting married on a cruise ship*' in your favourite search engine should reveal current information.

Clothes, accessories and beauty

I've included some information and ideas for hot climate versions of these topics in Chapter 4.

Photography

Similarly, I have included some advice for taking pictures in both snowy and hot, tropical conditions, in Chapter 7.

... do remember that different countries have different legal requirements in order for a marriage to be legally recognized in the UK so do get professional help in this area. Also, due to sometimes huge cultural differences, negotiations and service providers might need to be approached in a different way to those in the UK. Again, professional help is key here to ensure a successful wedding event.

Always check with your airline about luggage regulations and restrictions so that you can adequately plan for transportation of your dress etc.

If travelling as part of a group, remember to ask for discount – most airlines do offer this.

Check when rainy seasons, typhoon seasons etc. fall and try and avoid these times for your trip.

Many people forget that the Southern hemisphere summers can be uncomfortably hot for those of us used to the mild British summer so ensure that your accommodation has air-conditioning; take plenty of sunscreen, loose clothing and remember to drink plenty of fluids (water, not alcohol) to keep yourself feeling great and prevent dehydration.

Check that you have had all necessary immunizations and that you have a small supply of emergency medication (particularly if you suffer from a chronic illness) Try to avoid local school holiday periods as locals tend to swamp tourist sights at these times.

Lauren
The Wedding Connection
www.TheWeddingConnection.info

9 Planning a wedding in Western Europe

Austria

Austria in our cooler months is of course best known for its mountains and skiing opportunities. However its cities – Vienna and Salzburg in particular – are known to be very romantic all year round, although April and November are said to be the wettest months which could damp down proceedings somewhat. There is snow at low levels from December to March and earlier/later at higher levels, so if you're looking for a Winter Wonderland wedding setting Austria is a good bet. The run up to Christmas is quite spectacular in Austrian cities and towns, as it is in Germany, with lovely decorations and colourful Christmas markets. Woolly knickers are strongly advised, though – Austria is much colder in the winter months than the UK, whether you're up in the mountains or down in the valleys and cities.

Belgium

When I was researching for this book someone – a Belgian person, at that – asked me why on earth British people might want to get married in Belgium. I was quick to point out that despite not being on the worldwide map for much more than delicious 'pommes frites' and Hercule Poirot, Belgium has some gorgeous towns and cities as well as delightful, romantic rural settings. In the north of the country you have picturesque locations with beautiful architecture like Bruges, Antwerp and Brussels. In the south you can enjoy some wonderful woodland settings in the Ardennes in gorgeous chateaux, tucked away in the trees and hills with snow in the winter months as well as roaring open fires to keep you warm and cosy indoors. And everywhere in Belgium, the food is delicious. With some careful research you could create a magical wedding there and because it's not on the popular wedding trail, you could probably get some very good deals.

France

France in the cooler months can offer anything from a UK-like climate in the north, to snow and ice in the massif central and certainly plenty of that in its Alpine region, to balmy Mediterranean temperatures and weather in the south. Overall the weather tends to be unreliable everywhere at these times, even along the 'Cote d'Azur', so planning for a wedding to be outdoors-dependent is probably a bad idea. However you can be very lucky with the weather in France – luckier than in the UK – especially in the early autumn and mid-spring months.

The main advantages of France off-season are:

Price – there are some really excellent deals in very nice chateaux during the autumn and winter months.

The weather – often it's lovely here out of season and this can be true at any time of year, particularly in October and April.

The choice of suppliers is fantastic because unlike in the UK where weddings happen all year, in France there is a much shorter season so you have the pick of the bunch. As it is a tourist region you can find that some things are closed during parts of the winter but otherwise there are no disadvantages.

Beth Stretton
Get Married In France
www.getmarriedinfrance.co.uk

A significant advantage of France in the autumn, winter and spring is that this is a slower time for its tourist trade – yet many of the glorious chateaux, grand hotels, superb restaurants, etc. remain open if not for the whole period, most likely for some of it. Generally speaking they are glad to welcome out-of-season weddings business from British couples wishing to tie the knot there, and prices are much lower than at peak times.

That is almost certainly true of city venues, too — not just the rural chateaux and auberges. Paris and all the other large cities and towns are still lively through the off-peak tourist months and nearly every hotel and restaurant will be open for most of the time. However, prices here, just as in the countryside, are likely to be lower for the whole autumn/winter/spring period.

Germany

Not everyone is aware that Germany has more than 300 towns and resorts offering excellent winter sports facilities. And in the run-up to Christmas almost every town and city holds beautifully colourful and festive Christmas markets complete with glittering lights, mulled wine, spices and delicious food. As the markets start around the last week of November, an early December wedding in one of Germany's many attractive locations can be a lovely winter wonderland setting — especially if you pick one of its romantic castles and elegant, old fashioned hotels.

Beer lovers may prefer to arrange a wedding that coincides with one of Germany's beer festivals in the autumn months. And in the very south, you can think about a wedding along the well-known wine route — enjoying the grape harvesting in the autumn months, or gorgeous almond blossoms in the spring.

Germany, covering as it does such a large and varying area in weather terms, offers a surprisingly wide range of autumn, winter and spring wedding options with the added advantage that — at the time of writing, at least — its regulations concerning foreigners wishing to get married there are considerably less restrictive, by comparison, than those of Spain and France.

Ireland (Republic of)

In all honesty, Ireland is not going to head your list of wedding choices if you're looking for warm, sunny weather in the autumn, winter and spring months! However, there may be many other reasons why Ireland is a good choice for you, not least of which is the country's well-known charm and hospitality. Civil weddings are relatively easy to arrange there nowadays and an increasing number of attractive venues are being recognised as appropriate venues for a civil ceremony. As I've hinted, weather in Ireland is no better —

or at least, no dryer — than that of the UK in the cooler months, although many will tell you that it's milder over there in the winter, being warmed by close contact with the Gulf Stream.

Italy

I spent my first (April) honeymoon in Italy touring around Milan, Florence, Elba and Rome, and not only was it freezing cold, but also everything — including petrol stations and thereby hangs a tale — was shut for Easter. Despite that being back in the dark ages I think it's worth considering the fact that much of the romance and magic of Italy is dependent on its relationship with the sun and the great outdoors, and in the autumn, winter and spring months you can't depend on that although obviously temperatures are likely to be much milder than they are in the UK at the same time. If you're happy with an indoors-based wedding, however, Italy can offer some wonderful locations and with this being the off-peak season, such places as do remain open are likely to be offering bargains. Be warned, though (as I should have been) ... Christmas and Easter periods are not a good idea.

A great misconception that couples face when planning a wedding in Italy (or anywhere abroad) is they can create a wedding based on what a wedding concept, budget and style is in their native countries. A wedding abroad is not only a memorable wedding day that you and your guests will cherish forever but also an opportunity to embrace the culture and wedding traditions of the country you decide to get married in.

Deborah Taliani
Just get Married! Wedding Planners
www.justgetmarried.com

Netherlands

If you ask most people what the weather is like in the Netherlands during our autumn, winter and spring months, they're likely to burst out laughing and say, 'go somewhere else'. That may be true of less well-known regions of the

Netherlands but you should not discount the charm and ambience of the year-round Amsterdam, which offers tourists and bridal couples alike a fascinating range of options. Conventional romantics may choose to locate elsewhere (especially in these cold, damp months) but if you love Amsterdam's culture and rhythm, a wedding during its cooler months could be just what you need.

Portugal

Portugal is not the easiest of countries in which to have a legally-recognized wedding if you are both non-Portuguese citizens, although it's not impossible. Consequently, if this country is your choice it may be preferable to consider getting married at a Registry Office in the UK and then go to Portugal for a blessing and the main celebrations.

As for its climate, that of *the Algarve* (southern region) is delightful almost all year round, although the western end of the Algarve can get pretty windy, especially in the winter months, and obviously there is more rain through these months than there is in the summer. However even in the darkest of winter weeks the temperatures in the Algarve are pretty friendly to us northerners. A Portuguese friend of my son's — brilliant young golfer from Vilamoura — once complained to us of how cold it gets there in the winter. 'It can be really freezing', he shivered. 'It can get down as low as 10°C!'

Obviously this region is ideal if you, your partner and your wedding guests are keen golfers, as over half of the entire country's golf courses are located here and most of them are excellent. And there is an abundance of hotels offering good deals for autumn, winter and spring packages.

Further north, locations like *Lisbon* and *Porto* are very picturesque and offer some good packages in their off-peak seasons, too, but the weather is likely to be wetter and cooler than that of the Algarve.

Scandinavia

Obviously the Scandinavian countries have their own personalities and characteristics, but the common denominators through the cooler months of the year are cold, ice, snow, darkness, skiing, skating, etc.

One of the things that can put many people off the idea of visiting this part of the world in the northern hemisphere's autumn, winter and spring months is the fact that not only is it cold, but also dark most of the day. Whereas that's true — at the highest latitudes your hours of daylight dwindle to nothing for a good few weeks — it certainly doesn't seem to bother the Scandinavians very much, and there are still many attractions, of which admiring the Northern Lights is just one.

Some friends of mine spent a few days in Iceland between Christmas and New Year recently and had a wonderful time, skiing under floodlights and admiring that country's amazing countryside. Okay, in Iceland you do get a few hours of dim daylight in mid-winter but my friends said everything was so well organized that after the first day there, they didn't really notice how dark it was.

If you get married in these northern latitudes, you will obviously need either to time your wedding so that what natural daylight there is can be utilised to the full for outdoor pictures — or alternatively, organize photography that makes the most of the romantic, mysterious dusk. Red tape surrounding the legalities of foreigners getting married is relatively low in the Scandinavian countries, so they are quite a popular choice amongst bridal couples.

Denmark

Denmark in the cooler months may not be an ideal wedding location unless you have a specific reason to get married there, although the beauty and romance of *Copenhagen* certainly is breathtaking. From September, which is often a rainy month, the temperatures fall quite dramatically and by mid winter you can be looking at drop down to as little as −15° to −30°C. Snow is common, which makes things look pretty. As these months represent the low season in Denmark — especially mid-winter — prices in tourist venues should be low, assuming they're open at this time.

Finland

Finland, interestingly enough, has a relatively mild winter climate compared with other countries at this latitude, but be warned — I said 'relatively!' Even with the tempering influence of the Gulf Stream and other protective factors, temperatures in northern Finland can hit as low as −50°C, which is seriously cold. *Helsinki*, the capital, is an attractive city with a lot of beautiful architecture. As it has pretty dark days in the winter its lighting is creative and interesting, especially in the run-up to Christmas. If you're committed to cold, snow and skiing, there are useful opportunities for that further north.

Iceland

Iceland, as I mentioned above, is a country where no one seems to notice the dark winter days and tourism is, in fact, becoming almost as big in the winter months as it is at other times of the year. Despite being in quite a northerly location its climate, especially in lively *Reykjavik*, the capital, is relatively mild thanks to the proximity of the Gulf Stream. In Reykjavik the lowest winter temperatures tend not to drop much below freezing and snow is uncommon. Within a short drive, though, there are plenty of opportunities for both downhill and cross country skiing plus snowmobiling and various other winter sports. And swimming, both indoors and outdoors, takes place in pools using water heated naturally by the island's numerous hot springs.

Lapland

Lapland is a region, not a country; depending on who you ask, the region spreads across Finland, Sweden, Norway, and even Russia. Winter tourism here has become quite popular since the legend of Santa Claus placed his home in Lapland and pre-Christmas visits to Santa's workshops in Lapland have become quite a commercial goldmine. Also popular for winter sports, especially skiing, Lapland offers weddings in ice chapels and in the Swedish area, you can even stay in an ice hotel (http://www.icehotel.com). These structures are built in the late autumn, used by tourists, wedding parties, etc. through the winter months, then disappear altogether when the thaw comes in the spring. As the structures are understandably chilly, there is plenty of other accommodation available in charming wood chalets, hotels, and so-on where you can go and warm up.

Norway

Norway is another country with a climate − along the sea coast, anyway − that's milder than you would expect for somewhere so far north. Once again this is thanks to the Gulf Stream which swishes past Norway's miles and miles of fjord-punctuated coast. As the fjords and coast are backed by mountains, skiing is a very popular pastime here and the facilities attract quite a lot of foreign tourism. If you're not into skiing, the autumn months are very pleasant in Norway, as is the springtime. *Oslo*, its capital, is quite an interesting city but gets very cold from November through to March.

Whilst not being able to have the wedding outside ski resorts do have the allure of log cabins with fires in which to hold your wedding which work invariably well for smaller parties. Prices will be at their highest but the ability to ski before, after or maybe during a wedding stay could be the deciding factor.

James Lord
Love&Lord
www.loveandlord.com

Sweden

Sweden in the winter months tends to focus its tourism in the north of the country, especially with its ice hotel (see above). Other activities there include both downhill and cross country skiing, ice skating, ice fishing, ice yachting, reindeer and dog sleighing, etc. *Stockholm*, the capital, is a lively and interesting city which has become a popular gay venue in recent years. Like the other Scandinavian capitals, Stockholm's winter climate is quite cold.

Spain

At the time of writing, Spain is not a good choice for a legally-recognized marriage as for this to happen there is a compulsory residence requirement of two years. Please note that this may change, especially as I imagine the Spanish tourist industry is lobbying its government very hard to get that back down to a shorter timespan. Currently the advice is for couples either to do a Registry Office marriage in the UK, or – especially if they want their wedding celebrations to take place in south-western Spain — to do the Registry Office bit in Gibraltar, which as you know is a British territory. Then, you can arrange a blessing and all other celebrations in Spain itself.

Be aware of public holidays as in Spain they are taken seriously and everything can be closed.

Climate/Weather: as you know, this is very unpredictable but from October to January/February temperatures are the lowest of winter, from February to April can be much better, from 10°C and up.

Never forget the 'siesta' time from 2pm to 4pm where everything closes. Spain is a catholic country and in December from the 15th to January 6th, everything will be closed, including venues for weddings, so it's impossible to organize a wedding during this period.

Geraldine Borges
D'elite Spain Wedding Group
www.spain-wedding.com

Climate wise, in the autumn, winter and spring months the further south you go, the better the weather is likely to be. Eastern Spanish locations like *Barcelona* and *Valencia* can be quite miserable in winter although of course there are some glorious days. Prices at these out-of-season times tend to be very reasonable.

The main advantage of winter weddings in Granada is that it is not as hot as the summer months which can sometimes be too hot. Although the temperatures are lower, most days are sunny with beautiful blue skies. The venues have stunning views and these tend to be enhanced in winter as the area is much greener, and in the background you can see the snowy mountains of the Sierra Nevada.

The main disadvantage is that the weather is not predictable and there is a higher chance of rain. This can eliminate the use of some venues that do not have wet weather contingencies or increase the cost as a marquee would need to be hired. Having said that, most venues do have indoor spaces in case of bad weather.

Theresa Guthrie
AWOL in Granada
www.awolgranada.com

Switzerland

It seems that at the time of writing, at least, Switzerland is not a difficult place in red-tape terms for foreigners to marry, and if a sophisticated picture post-card backdrop is what you want you really couldn't pick a better country, whatever the time of year. Unfortunately Switzerland is not cheap, but offers some wonderful cities, lakeside towns, and of course mountain resorts with delicious food, pure, clean air and a pretty fair dose of reasonable weather even in the cooler months. In the autumn and spring you do risk some rain, but in the spring, when vegetation and the countryside generally are bursting into life, the lower levels and lakesides are really beautiful. The ski season can be quite long, with resorts opening late November until April.

10 Planning a wedding in Eastern Europe and the Mediterranean

Baltic States

Strictly speaking we shouldn't really refer to the countries of *Estonia*, *Latvia* and *Lithuania* as 'the Baltic states' any more since they joined the EU in 2004 as individual countries in their own right. Unfortunately, as far as I can gather, winter comes fairly early (mid-November) and spring rather late (late March to early April), and the winters can be pretty damp and chilly although not always very cold. However, you may be compensated for this as the tourism industry in these countries is growing by leaps and bounds, not least because of the stunning, romantic Baroque architecture and heritage of their capital cities and the very good-value prices of accommodation, dining, nightlife, etc.

Bulgaria

Bulgaria is a beautiful country and in the last few years has become inundated with foreigners keen to take advantage of its pleasant climate, attractive sur-roundings and low property prices. Apart from this it also offers some excellent winter sports opportunities in the mountainous region at prices gen-erally lower than those of France, Switzerland, etc. Winters are surprisingly cool even in the southern region and at sea level, although autumn and spring can be very pleasant.

Cyprus

Cyprus is a lovely island and its climate from October through to March is very pleasant indeed. Even in their very short winter from late December to early February, their weather is said to be like that of a pleasant British spring. And yet despite this balmy climate around the coast, up in the Troodos Mountains a mere short drive away there is sometimes enough snow for skiing in the winter months. It's said that there are well over 300 days of sunshine in Cyprus every year which makes it an attractive choice for an autumn, winter or spring wedding; the coldest average daytime temperature is over 15°C in January and February, with November, December and March hovering around 20°C and October up around 25°C. With the cooler months being the low season in Cyprus, you may well find some good deals, especially in terms of hotel or self-catering accommodation for your guests.

Czech Republic

As you probably know the Czech Republic's capital city, *Prague*, is becoming an increasingly popular destination for tourism — whether for holidaymakers, stag/hen celebrations, weekend breakers, wedding parties or honeymooners. Its autumn, winter and spring climate is pretty cold; daytime temperatures in midwinter are hard pushed to creep over 0°C, and it's all downwards from there at night. However, the winters are relatively dry — it seems the Czech Republic gets higher rainfall in the spring and summer months. If you're looking for a winter wonderland setting for your wedding, there's plenty of snow in midwinter in the country generally, although Prague itself tends not to get so much. It's reasonable to assume that, this being the low season for tourism, prices in Prague for accommodation and reception venues should be pretty reasonable, but it's also possible that some venues will be closed for the winter.

Greece

In Greece the autumn and spring months can be delightful, but also can be wet, especially in the northern bit of the Ionian region. *Corfu* is known as one of the greenest islands in Greece which is lovely, but of course the reason why it is so green is because it rains there quite a lot.

Northern Greece can actually be quite cold in the winter months, with ice and snow, and because of this most of that region tends to close down so is not a particularly good choice for a cooler-months wedding.

The southern areas enjoy a more moderate climate and islands like *Crete* and *Rhodes* offer not only a reasonably warm and friendly climate during these months, but also are more likely to offer venues that stay open year round – or at least for most of that period.

Getting married in the *smaller islands* during the winter months may be a bit tricky as many venues in these islands are likely to be closed. Autumn and spring months, however, may not be so much of a problem.

On the mainland, *Athens*, the country's capital, is a bustling city year-round and offers all the obvious amenities of major international hub with the added advantages of incredibly fascinating history, culture, architecture and more. In fact many people say that life in Athens is at its best and liveliest in the autumn, winter and spring months when it's not packed out with tourists. Christmas and Easter (Greek Orthodox Easter, which is usually at least one week later than the UK Easter) are busy times, as is Apokreas, the winter carnival that takes place late January to early February. However, these periods do not necessarily mean that a wedding can't be arranged.

Hungary

Hungary is a chilly option in our cooler months, but you may well be compensated here by the beauty of *Budapest* which has been called the 'Paris of the East' as well as the 'Pearl of the Danube.' The winter months see very low temperatures and frequent snow, although heavy snowfalls are not frequent. There's quite a lot going on in the autumn, winter and spring months in terms of music and other cultural activities as well as wine festivals and a wide selection of colourful Christmas fairs throughout December.

Israel

Israel obviously holds many attractions for Jewish couples, and bear in mind that in some circumstances Muslim and Christian weddings can take place there too. Officially Israel is a secular country and can accommodate weddings of all faiths. However, it's worth remembering that at the time of writing (mid-2008) if you are Jewish and wish to marry in Israel you will need to be aware of the Orthodox-only circumstances which are current.

For up-to-date information, key '***marriages+Israel***' into your favourite search engine.

Whereas summer months can prove hot and sweaty, autumn and spring months in Israel are truly delightful and even the winter months, although on the cool side for this part of the world, only produce a relatively few days of rainfall each season.

Eilat, in particular, based on the Red Sea coast, is a popular resort for everyone throughout the year and is especially prized as a location for honeymoons, at least, in our winter months. Being located to the extreme south of Israel it enjoys a warm climate and being very dry, offers a climate which year round is very pleasant. Snorkelling and diving are popular activities there and give visitors the opportunity to see some outstanding underwater wildlife.

Malta

Malta is one of those destinations that sometimes can be overlooked for a wedding option, but in truth its archipelago of three islands represents a lovely place to consider. It has a vibrant history and very interesting culture to combine with a pleasant climate, located as it is roughly halfway across the Mediterranean between Italy and Libya. Winters in Malta tend to be very mild with temperatures seldom falling below the mid teens Celsius, and according to many of its descriptive websites its temperatures remain very civilized, especially in October and November where the high 20s Celsius are common and sunshine is expected daily.

Poland

Poland in the winter months is pretty cold and snowy, so if it's a Winter Wonderland you're looking for this is a candidate. The main cities like *Warsaw* and *Krakow* offer some interesting architecture and places to visit. Skiing is very popular in the southern, mountainous region of Poland and the spring months are said to be very attractive with the scent of blossoms perfuming the air. I haven't been to Poland but looking at some sample prices of accommodation, dining, etc., it would seem that you can get pretty good value for money there.

Romania

Of all the countries in this region, Romania probably has the most in terms of romantic association — the connection with Count Dracula and Transylvania being just one of many, along with beautiful scenery, fascinating architecture, colourful traditions and culture, mysterious castles, fortresses and more. I haven't been there but I'm told that *Bucharest* is an interesting city full of French neo-classical buildings, elegant parks, old-fashioned streets and alleys, contrasted by the enormous Parliament Palace — a relic from the era of the dictator, Ceausescu — which, with a floor area of more than 3.75 million square feet is the second largest building in the world (the largest is the Pentagon in the USA). The four seasons in Romania are said to compare with those of north-eastern United States, with cold, snowy winters but colourful vegetation with the turning leaves in the autumn, and fresh, pleasant daytime temperatures in the spring.

Russia

Some would say that any British couple choosing Russia as a wedding location is asking for a very complex and red-tape-ridden time, but as far as I can make out technically it is possible, at the time of writing, for British people to marry there, especially if the other partner is Russian. The climate in the winter months in Russia is notoriously cold and snowy (and autumn and spring can be chilly too) but the romantic architecture, culture and traditions in cities like Moscow and St Petersburg can provide a superb Winter Wonderland backdrop for a wedding with a real difference. Just remember to pack your woolly underwear.

Slovakia

Slovakia's history as Slovakia is fairly recent, as it only split from the Czech Republic in 1993. I'm told it's a jolly, picturesque, delightfully unspoilt country with lovely, romantic towns and plenty of winter sports opportunities in its mountainous region, which would make it worth considering for a skiing-orientated wedding celebration. It seems tourism to Slovakia is growing very quickly, but at the time of writing, prices still represent pretty good value. If you're not a skier, the autumn and spring months are said to be good times to visit, with the autumn tending to be the driest period. Winter brings snow from November to May in the Tatras mountains, so there is a good ski season there.

Turkey

I'm told that the winter months are not a good time to contemplate a wedding in Turkey because not only is the weather surprisingly unfriendly — cold, wet and even snowy — but also many of the coastal towns and resorts close down for the period. Autumn and spring, however, are much more agreeable in weather terms and resorts are more likely to be open. In addition, you won't get the crowds typical of the summer months, plus you will get better prices.

Former Yugoslavian countries

As everyone knows this region went through a great deal of turmoil in the early 1990s but in more recent times has emerged — and in some cases, re-emerged — as an excellent tourist region and one where unusual and memorable weddings can be arranged. *Slovenia* offers very good skiing at reasonable prices, with the added attractions of major ski competitions in January and March — and if you're there in the late spring, you'll see some beautiful blossoming vegetation. *Bosnia and Herzegovina* also offers excellent skiing and resorts; *Sarajevo* hosted the winter Olympics there in 1984. *Croatia* has some gorgeous coastline and is very popular amongst sailors and divers in the summer months. Autumn and winter months can be rainy there, but spring is a good time to enjoy the sights without the crowds, and before temperatures get too high.

11 Planning a wedding in the Americas

Canada

Canada is known for its cold winters and certainly this is not the country to choose for a winter beach wedding! The early autumn is a lovely time in many parts, with beautiful brash colours of the turning leaves and crisp, clear sunny days. Canada is also becoming very popular with skiers, not only in the Rockies but also in Quebec — Mont Tremblant (http://www.tremblant.ca) is an extremely well appointed ski resort — and even in Ontario a mere two hours north of Toronto, at Blue Mountain (http://www.bluemountain.ca) which is another purpose-built ski and leisure complex. The ski season runs from December to March.

Another unusual wedding offering in Canada is the Ice Hotel, near Quebec City. You'll need your woolly lingerie under your wedding attire, but I'm assured that getting married here is an amazing experience. You can see more on their website, at: http://www.icehotel-canada.com.

Caribbean

What can I say about the Caribbean in our cooler months that hasn't already been said many times over — it's the best time of the year to visit this area, by far. Rainfall is minimal, the hurricane season is over (well, nearly — it normally finishes around November) and the sun shines in temperatures that are warm without being suffocatingly hot or humid. Naturally prices reflect these idyllic circumstances, especially over the Christmas and New Year period, but there are locations where you can get much more reasonable deals. These tend to be islands and resorts which are not on the mainstream tourist trail. There are many specialist companies offering wedding packages to the whole of the Caribbean area and it really does pay to shop around, even for deals at the peak tourist times. To find them, key '***getting married in the Caribbean***' into your favourite search engine.

Central America

The Central American countries of *Belize, Costa Rica, El Salvador, Guatemala, Honduras, Nicaragua and Panama* are largely tropical and subtropical in climate, with a few temperate areas mainly higher up in altitude. Many parts are very hot and humid and their rainy season is quite long, but at least the months of December/January to April/May are fairly dry. The official language of Belize is English – formerly it was British Honduras – but English is quite widely spoken in the other countries, too. As this part of the world is not (yet) a well-known location for weddings and wedding-related tourism, it's probably better to consult specialist tour operators rather than DIY where your arrangements are concerned. A helpful place to start looking is: http://centralamerica.com.

Mexico

Oh, what a popular place Mexico has become through the autumn and spring months, and especially the winter months when the sun-starved North Americans hit it in droves to escape the snow, ice and other issues they're obliged to deal with at their northern latitudes. As a wedding destination Mexico is also popular, particularly as at the time of writing, at least, its legal requirements for the marriage of foreigners are relatively simple. (Please note: these can change!) Mexico obviously offers a wide variety of touristic options ranging from beach locations to those involved with the country's long and interesting history. It's a long way from the UK, but it offers wonderful wedding opportunities.

South America

It seems disrespectful in a way to lump all of these magnificent countries together under one heading, especially as being a large continent South America offers everything from soup to nuts in terms of weather and climate during our autumn, winter and spring months. As you know most of it is in the southern hemisphere, so seasons are reversed.

As for the weather conditions during our cooler months, most of South America is enjoying its spring, summer and autumn, so in general a wedding planned at this time is likely to be blessed by sunshine and warm temperatures.

Judging from what I've found in my research the red tape factor concerning British couples getting married in some South American countries is not too awful. However, bear in mind that even with the help of a specialized foreign wedding consultant things are going to be that much more complex than were you to choose a country for your wedding that's closer to home.

Bear in mind, for what it's worth, that Spanish is the principal language spoken everywhere in South America *except* in Brazil, where the main language is Portuguese.

Argentina

In *Argentina*, you'll find that weather in *Buenos Aires* goes from mild to hot to mild again through the cooler months, and this is the best time of the year to visit beautiful *Patagonia*, as during its winter months it gets very cold. Overall, Argentina is a fascinating country and one which I would love to see. Maybe one day.

Brazil

In *Brazil* you have a wide range of climates in one country. *Sao Paolo* is likely to be warm and wet during these months. *Rio de Janeiro* is hot and humid. Bear in mind that although the Brazilian Mardi Gras celebrations just prior to Lent are a wonderful time to visit with exotic and brilliantly colourful activities going on for days, this may not be the ideal time to choose for your wedding which could get totally overwhelmed by the general festivities. Also, it may well be hard to book accommodation and a venue – plus the fact that this will be Brazil's high – i.e. expensive – season.

Chile

Chile is the long, thin streak of a country squashed between the Pacific Ocean and the Andes mountains running down South America's south-west coast. One of its finest exports is its wine, which certainly can give the produce of

Australia, New Zealand, California and Europe a run for its money. As a destination to visit between October and March, the timing couldn't be better, but
bear in mind that temperatures vary considerably from the north to the south,
and from sea level to the mountain tops.

Ecuador

Ecuador would not ordinarily deserve a mention here as I'm only touching on
the larger South American countries, but it has something the other countries
don't have – the *Galapagos*. *Quito*, the capital city, is almost bang on the
equator (25 miles away) so you would expect it to be warm. However, it is
also at an altitude of just under 3,000 metres, which means you get fairly cool
weather when it's cloudy and hot sun when the clouds disperse. It's such a
weird climate that you get rose bushes (temperate) growing next to huge
cactus plants (tropical) – I know, because I've seen them! *Guayaquil* is on the
coast and so has a much hotter, more humid climate and this is the jumping
off point for most of the tours to the Galapagos Islands. Both Quito and
Guayaquil experience their rainy seasons in our cooler months, unfortunately,
but the Galapagos is said to have a magical, dry climate with an average daytime temperature of around 25°C, year round.

Peru

Peru, as you know, is home to the much-trodden-upon-by-tourists *Machu
Picchu* along with various other relics of the country's ancient history, and I'm
told *Lima* is a bustling, interesting city. The coastal area, including Lima, is
warm and dry nearly all year round with very little rainfall. If you are going
up into the highlands, though, bear in mind that October to April is their wet
season – sorry about that.

United States

Although the USA is vast, its attributes are very well known, so I don't need to
give you the basics about the country. Overall, marriage between foreigners
seems relatively straightforward in red-tape terms, so to give you some
guidelines I've sectioned the country off into quarters and made my suggestions about places you might like to consider for a cooler-months wedding.

North-east USA

North-east USA, generally speaking, is loveliest in the autumn months when the 'fall' colours are at their best and the temperatures are pleasantly warm during the day, if a bit chilly by night. Springtime tends to be pretty short and sharp after a long, snowy winter. *Boston* is an attractive city that's at its best in the autumn and late spring months — a wonderful place if you like attractive architecture, good shopping and delicious seafood. *New York City* is good fun anywhere from October to March and the run-up to Christmas is very exciting, with gorgeous decorations everywhere and incredible shopping as well as all the other usual attractions. *Chicago*, on Lake Michigan, is also an interesting city but can get very cold in the winter.

South-east USA

South-east USA is at its best during our cooler months and although many of the states there do have a winter, it tends to be very short — December and January only. I spent a few weeks working in Georgia and Tennessee some years back during October and November and the daytime temperatures were well up into the 20s. Obviously *Florida* is included in this region and its weather is very warm in the south and usually warm and dry — but not always — in northern areas on both the Atlantic and Gulf coasts. *New Orleans* is usually very pleasant even in the winter months with average daily highs of around 15°C — and it's a beautiful city again now, as much of its glory is being restored after their disastrous Hurricane Katrina in 2005. (NB that occurred in August.) Obviously, avoid the hurricane season which can drag on into November.

South-west USA

South-west USA is also at its best during our cooler months as their summers, like those of most of the rest of the country, can be pretty hot. *Texas*, being so large, has a range of climates and winters in the northern part of the state get cold, with some snow. *Houston* on the Gulf coast has mild winters and pleasant autumns and springs, but early autumn is best avoided as this is the latter part of the hurricane season. Moving west, **Arizona** is extremely pleasant during the autumn, winter and spring months, as well as being relatively dry. Consequently, this is a peak tourism time here. If you want glamorous, sophisticated skiing, travel north to *Colorado* where resorts like *Aspen* and the city of *Denver* make a gorgeous, if pricey, setting for a Winter Wonderland wedding. Travelling west again, the state of *Nevada* beckons with all the wedding glitz you expect in *Las Vegas* where even mid-winter daytime temperatures are in the comfortable mid-teens Celsius and there is little rain. (NB It's one of life's little ironies that whereas Las Vegas is known as the wedding capital of the USA, *Reno*, also in Nevada and a mere few hundred miles away, is the divorce capital.) Heading west again we arrive at *California* and the Pacific Ocean. Although some people expect southern California to be perpetually hot and sunny, the coastal area is tempered by breezes and mists from the ocean, leaving the climate pleasantly warm in our cooler months with temperatures rarely dropping below 12°C from *San Diego* through *Los Angeles* and northwards. Once you get to *San Francisco* you'll find it tends to be damper, although winter temperatures hold up pretty well.

North-west USA

North-west USA starts with the delightful wine-making region of northern California, or at least the part that leads north from San Francisco towards *Oregon*. Also in this region you can see the glorious ancient redwood trees, the Yosemite in the Sierra Nevada and even enjoy a skiing break at Lake Tahoe just over the Nevada state line. Autumn and spring months are particularly good times for sightseeing, and the autumn months are ideal for wine lovers. Oregon is also a wine-making state and offers surprisingly good skiing, as does *Washington State* – and a ski-based wedding celebration in these states is likely to be less costly than in trendy Colorado. It's easy to get flights from the UK to Seattle (Washington), although at the time of writing you need to go via another European hub, e.g. Amsterdam, to Portland (Oregon).

Hawaii

As you probably know, Hawaii consists of an archipelago of romantic, sun-kissed islands which have been glamorized by Hollywood movies even before they became the 49th United State in 1959. There can be no disputing the islands' beauty or warm climate; temperatures during the day from October to March are in the very comfortable high 20s, and if you stick to the leeward side of the archipelago (south-west) you're likely to find a dryish climate year round.

Not surprisingly, as a card-carrying US state, many parts of Hawaii have become very commercialized, and somewhat pricey — especially if you knit in the cost of travelling there which for those of us in the UK, as near as dammit amounts to travelling half-way around the world. Our cooler months, as in the case of those of most of the US, are very popular times to visit Hawaii, so if this is the wedding venue of your dreams forget bargains. But as for romance, well — who could find a better venue than that of all those ultra-cheesy movies? (And believe me, at the time of writing they still do all the grass skirts, leis, and Hawaiian guitar stuff.)

Alaska

Alaska — in our cooler months? Are we being serious here? Well, it seems that contrary to what we would assume, Alaska does not close down from October onwards for a few months, but actually enjoys some interesting activities and temperatures that are not necessarily going to give you instant frostbite. In fact Alaska, at the time of writing appears to offer some interesting winter wedding options including a ceremony on a glacier, via helicopter of course, with — perhaps — celebrations continuing in what they call 'glacier gardens' plus horse or dog drawn sleighing, skiing, snowboarding, hockey, ice skating, ice fishing, and a host of winter festivals and other celebrations. They claim their minimum number of daily daylight hours in our winter is six, so at least you can see where you're going without artificial help for a while, and according to them the surrounding hours of beautiful twilight and dawns really do make up for the lack of sun in your face.

12 Planning a wedding in Africa, India and Indian Ocean

Africa, north

Egypt

In Egypt, the weather is pleasant in the winter months with an average minimum daytime temperature of 14°–18°C, depending on where you are, although it can get much warmer than that during the day. The desert areas can get down as low as freezing (0°C) at night. October can still be quite warm or even hot. Humidity and rainfall are both low in the cooler months, so it's a pleasant place to consider. It might be better to avoid March, April and even May, though, as the sirocco winds common at that time can whip up nasty sandstorms. The climate in Cairo is particularly dry – it gets less than an inch of rain per year, and through the cooler months the humidity is down, too.

The coastal areas of *Tunisia* get an average of at least six hours sun per day in winter, and have a typical 'Mediterranean' climate. Temperatures in those areas rarely fall below 10°C and can get up as high as 30°C. What rain there is tends to fall in short showers and it clears away again pretty soon. The weather will be colder if you venture up into the mountains inland. The spring months are particularly appealing, with a host of colourful wild flowers to admire – and perhaps to incorporate into your wedding plans.

Algeria

Algeria is also mild but can get some rain from November to March. Temperatures are mild in the north, without much of a difference between night and day.

Morocco

Morocco has a subtropical climate, and can get additional winter weather problems storming across from the Atlantic. However, in the Marrakech area the average daytime winter temperature is around 20°C — very pleasant! The main tourist areas can be rainy in the cooler months, however.

> A destination like Morocco ... will still have a good climate in the winter and it may be the best time of year as the summer temperatures in these countries can be unbearably hot. These months are invariably cheaper than the summer months as the tourist influx is reduced. There is also a good chance that your date and venue will be available and can be booked later than a summer date. Plus you can probably still have the event outside.
>
> **James Lord**
> **Love&Lord**
> **www.loveandlord.com**

Canaries

The Canaries enjoy a mild to warm climate pretty much year round, and although you can get rain showers coming from the Atlantic systems in winter months they're usually not too serious or long-lived. Average daytime temperatures in the winter months are in the high teens, which is quite pleasant for a wedding celebration. However, because the Canaries are part of Spain their regulations on marriages between foreigners are as awkward as those of the mainland, so perhaps these islands are best reserved for a blessing, or just for your honeymoon.

Africa, east

Kenya

Kenya is absolutely delightful in our cooler months — in fact this is definitely the best time of year to visit most of East Africa. The temperatures can go pretty high and humidity along the coast can be high, too, although inland is drier and not so stuffy. You may get the occasional 'tropical' rain shower in October and November – one of their rainy seasons – but any such showers will tend to be short and the sun will soon be shining again. The main Kenyan rainy season is from April to June.

Nairobi

Nairobi, the capital, is inland and at quite high altitude, so the climate is very warm and pleasant most of the time through our winter (their summer) months. However the weather can get a bit cloudy and damp in February and March.

Mombasa

Mombasa, on the Indian Ocean coast, tends to be hotter and more humid. You do get some respite from the delightful sea breezes, and of course with such a highly developed tourist industry along this coast, air-conditioning is available very widely. Prices will tend to be quite high at this time, especially over the Christmas and New Year period when northern Europeans flock here in their thousands. However, if you avoid December and January, better deals may well be found.

Tanzania

Tanzania is a little further south of the equator and so its climate tends more towards that of the southern hemisphere. Its main rainy season is roughly from March through to May, with awe-inspiring tropical downpours in the afternoons. Not surprisingly the humidity is high at this time too, making movement outdoors rather uncomfortable, especially when the temperatures go as high as 35°C or so. October is at the end of their dry season and usually is very pleasant, but once you get into November and December you hit another rainy season. This, like the rainy season at the same time in Kenya, tends to be less spectacular and what showers occur are fairly light and short-lived. In January and February, the weather tends to be dry again.

The weather in *Zanzibar* is similar to that of Tanzania, although it can be slightly more humid. Also the high temperatures of their summer months (our winter months) are cooled slightly by the breezes from the Indian Ocean.

Africa, south

South Africa

South Africa is enjoying its own summer during our cooler months so temperatures will tend to be high, but inland and in most areas there will be rain and thunderstorms in the afternoons. These, however, tend not to last very long and clear away to reveal hot sunshine again. Sunshine hours are long pretty well everywhere in the country except in the Western Cape area, which has a climate more like that of our Mediterranean and tends to get its heavy rain in the South African winter months.

Generally speaking, the South African spring (our autumn months) and autumn (our spring months) are said to be the best time to visit the country. And as temperatures are not too high and rainfall is pretty low, these are good months to contemplate wedding celebrations over there.

Much of the Capetown area has an excellent climate from October to March and is very popular with both South African and foreign holidaymakers, so this may well be an expensive time to consider a wedding there. Once again the Christmas and New Year period is very busy with prices to match, but further away from this period prices can moderate.

Botswana

Botswana does not offer especially good weather conditions from December to March, as this is a predominantly rainy season. Temperatures are warm rather than very hot and of course there are sunny days, but those are punctuated by cloudy periods and afternoon thunderstorms. April is a good month to visit Botswana, though, although the weather can be cool. September and October can be very hot, and are generally said to be the best months for game safaris.

Namibia

Namibia has a pleasant, dry climate, although you can get some humidity and local thunderstorms in the afternoons through the months of December to March. Like Botswana, the months of April, September and October are good choices for a wedding visit, with September and October offering a good – if sometimes dusty – chance to see wildlife at its best.

Africa, west

Senegal

Senegal has a dry season that goes from December to April and beyond, with warm weather fanned on the coast by trade winds. Much of the rest of the year the weather tends to be hot and humid, so wedding plans for Senegal are probably best made during these months.

The Gambia

The Gambia has a lovely climate with very warm, sunny weather for most of the year. Our autumn, winter and spring months are definitely the best time to enjoy the Gambia and in the winter months, temperatures actually drop to what we would call 'cool' levels at night, which most of us northern folks appreciate. The Gambia also offers some very pleasant resorts at reasonable prices, although with the country having become very popular as a tourist destination in recent years, it's possible that bargains are not quite as easy to find as they used to be.

Cape Verde

At the time of writing, Cape Verde is what our current tourism and wedding tourism trade would call a 'developing venue'. Essentially, Cape Verde – if you don't know it already – consists of an archipelago of islands in the Atlantic Ocean west of Senegal which are becoming more and more interesting to us lot up here in northern Europe as a good-value tourism spot, and also, of course, as a wedding location. This archipelago, which was colonized originally by the Portuguese, consists basically of volcanic islands which enjoy a year-round tropical climate tempered, as they are, by breezes from the Atlantic. Average temperatures during our cooler months run around the mid-20s in January. Their rainy season is said to be during the months of August to October, so if you're looking at a wedding there November onwards would appear to be a better bet.

India

Perhaps helped by the rapid spread of Bollywood culture around the world and Elizabeth Hurley's widely publicized nuptials there, India is becoming a very popular destination not only for tourism, but also for weddings. With the autumn, winter and spring months representing the most favourable times of year weather-wise for us northerners, plus an incredibly diverse choice of romantic locations, you can understand why India is gaining this useful chunk of international weddings business. At the time of writing, there is a fairly long compulsory residence period for foreigners but the Indian tourist trade is lobbying hard for that to change, so it's easier for foreign couples to turn up and get wed. Already there are numerous specialist wedding tour operators offering packages, which you'll find by entering '***getting married in India***' into your favourite search engine.

Indian Ocean

This region is well-known as the dream holiday area of the world in our cooler months, so although having your wedding here is bound to be stunning, don't expect many discounts as this is peak tourist season. Expect glorious sandy beaches, tropical vegetation with palm trees and picture-postcard sunsets – everything you need for a beautiful wedding with your honeymoon on the doorstep.

The Maldives

The Maldives are located a relatively short way to the south-west of the southern tip of India, and of Sri Lanka. A predominantly Muslim country, the Maldives consists of nearly 1,200 islands, most of which are uninhabited. Being very close to the equator the climate is pretty hot all year round, but with a long-running wet season from April to October, our late autumn, winter and spring months are the best time to visit. Not surprisingly the resorts and accommodation tend to get booked up quickly, so if you're thinking of having your wedding here, plan well ahead.

Mauritius

Mauritius is yet another idyllic island nation, to the east of Madagascar and Mozambique off the south-east African coast. Being south of the equator its best time for visits is during its winter, i.e. our summer, but even during its hot summer months the temperatures are cooled by the sea breezes. It would seem that November, December and April are likely to offer the most pleasant weather; from January to March you can get cyclones with rain and high winds, although on average there aren't many of them and they tend only to last a couple of days.

The Seychelles

The Seychelles is perhaps the best known of all the Indian Ocean island nations, located just south of the equator almost directly east of the Kenya coast. Temperatures here vary between the low 20s and low 30s. This time of the year is slightly warmer than in our summer months, and January and February should perhaps be avoided as this is when the tropical rains come.

Sri Lanka

Sri Lanka, like many tourist locations in this region, was badly affected by the tsunami in 2004, but has now been appropriately rebuilt. Some people may feel a little reluctant to go there due to Sri Lanka's ongoing political internal issues. However as a wedding venue, it offers a huge amount of character, history, culture and tradition along with the more usual requisites of sun, sand and sea. Although the climate is very warm with an average year-round high daytime score of just under 30°C, you can get heavy monsoon rains anywhere from October to January, depending on where you are. So this may be better considered for a spring wedding.

13 Planning a wedding in the Middle East, Far East, Australia and New Zealand

Australia

The climate in Australia is generally warm and pleasant — just with some parts warmer and pleasanter than others!

The best location for a wedding would be Australia. In fact, between October and April is spring and summer, the best time of the year here. The only disadvantage may be the distance if a couple is not willing to travel that far for a wedding. During these months it is better to avoid any ceremonies between 11am and 4pm as it is very hot. Also the couple should pay attention to the weather and wear sunscreen prior the wedding and on the wedding day. This is to avoid to turning up on their wedding burnt and/or with tan lines (horrible ... we've seen so many brides making this mistake over and over again!)

Deborah Taliani
Just get Married! Wedding Planners
www.justgetmarried.com

The northern part of the country — in fact roughly the northern two-thirds of it — tends to be very hot and humid, whereas the southern part is very pleasant during the months of October to April. If you want to venture to the northern parts, the best of our cooler months to choose are September, October and November. The other months (December to April) can be quite rainy. In the south, however, the climate is usually very friendly, with average daytime temperatures ranging from the mid to high teens in September, October and November up to the low to mid-20s through to March in Perth, Sydney, and Brisbane. Average daily temperatures are said to be somewhat cooler in Adelaide, Melbourne and Hobart (Tasmania).

Bahrain

Bahrain is one of the Persian Gulf destinations and as such is definitely not somewhere within our northern comfort zones in the summer months. However, its climate during our autumn and spring months is very pleasant with almost guaranteed sunshine without temperatures that will melt precious metals — and in fact during the winter months the weather can become quite cool, and rainy. Prices at this time of year are not low, but the main Bahrain Island and the capital, *Manama*, offer plenty of exotic things to do and see and certainly would make an interesting wedding venue. Regulations on alcohol are generally more easy-going here than in other Arab countries.

China

At the time of writing, for foreigners to marry in China is not what you'd call straightforward, although — as far as I can see — it's not impossible in some circumstances, primarily if one of the partners is Chinese. By the time you read this, though, regulations concerning marriages between foreigners may well have relaxed. And what an unusual and fascinating venue for a wedding! Realistically, for UK brides and grooms it may be more practical to confine wedding ambitions to the main cities of Beijing and Shanghai, but please remember that this is likely to change and expand dramatically. Writing this as I do can only represent a current (mid-2008) snapshot of the way things are, and hopefully over the coming shelf life of this book more and more of China will open up as a potential wedding venue.

Beijing experiences a cold period during our winter months, although the early autumn months are said to be lovely and spring, from February to April, is supposed to be warm though windy. Similarly, the autumn and spring months are said to be the best times to visit Shanghai, but the winter months can be very cold and unfriendly.

And as for China as an out-of-season wedding destination overall? Definitely there are options on the horizon that are really thrilling, but at the time I'm writing this book it's a case of 'watch and wait'.

Far East

The Far East covers a number of popular tourist regions and our autumn, winter and spring months are probably a better time to contemplate a wedding celebration there, overall, than in the heat of the summer. Because in general the weather may be friendlier in these months, prices may be correspondingly higher than when their weather is too hot/wet/humid/etc. However, this is your wedding, so it's a good time to spoil yourselves!

Hong Kong

Hong Kong, despite its change of status from British ownership to Chinese in 1997, is still a rich mixture of cultures, wonderful shopping, delicious food and exciting things to do. The average highest temperatures from October to March range from the high teens to the mid 20s, but can go down as low as 14°C or 15°C in December, January and February. The best months to choose for a wedding celebration would be November, December, March or April.

Indonesia

Indonesia (including Bali) has a mainly tropical climate, and may not be an ideal choice for a wedding during our cooler months. That's because their rainy season runs from December to March and from September to December, you run the risk of experiencing typhoons. However, as this is not the best tourist season it may be possible to find good deals, even in the most popular areas.

Malaysia/Singapore

Malaysia/Singapore, being geographically very close to Indonesia, have a similar climate. Their rainy seasons are slightly different, with the west side experiencing theirs between September and December, and the east side from October to February. The monsoon season runs from November to February. However, March and April appear to be good times to visit.

Thailand

Thailand, on the other hand, is a far better bet in weather terms during our cooler months. Their dry season runs from November to February, and is also Thailand's coolest time of the year. However don't be fooled by their interpretation of 'cool' — daytime temperatures in Bangkok can still reach the mid-30s. September and October are probably best avoided as this is the end of the monsoon season and you can get quite severe flooding. And once you get into March temperatures begin to climb steeply.

Japan

Japan can actually be quite cold in our autumn, winter and spring months — in fact during the winter, skiing is a popular pastime. However, some say that the Japanese aren't very good at organizing good heating in the winter months and a visit there at that time may well be somewhat chilly. Autumn and spring are said to be the best times to visit Japan, and to arrange a wedding there. Needless to say it offers an incredibly different, exciting and romantic range of options for UK bridal couples.

New Zealand

Some people view New Zealand as something of an 'also ran' in terms of tourism to the Antipodes. Being a Canadian and so a similarly afflicted victim of a country seen as an 'also ran' (in our case, vis à vis the USA), I have to say I understand the New Zealanders' irritation at being compared with their larger, richer neighbours. Not to worry. New Zealand is a fascinating, unique country that offers unbelievable variety in terms of culture, countryside, climate — you name it.

As a venue for a wedding, New Zealand offers a stunning range of options year round. You can even ski in our summer months, but of course this is not what we're talking about in this book. Our autumn, winter and spring months are — as you know — their spring, summer and autumn months, so represent an excellent time of year.

New Zealand offers a very wide range of climatic ambiences despite its relatively small size. Whereas in the north of the north island you experience warm sub-tropical weather, at the south end of the south island you can get all the force and fury of the Antarctic. Also, I'm told that October and November can experience high winds in the south island, and stormy rain in the northern parts.

Overall, however, New Zealand's summer temperatures (i.e. those during our winter months) tend to run from a very agreeable teens to low 30s. The best months of all are January, February and March – but it appears that many businesses and hotels close down from around 24 December to 2 January, so a Christmas or New Year wedding may not be a good choice here.

Oman

Oman does offer wedding packages for foreigners, at a price. However, if you can afford it this is an interesting and romantic part of the world, particularly in the main city of *Muscat*. The climate here in the summer months is unbearably scorching but in our autumn, winter and spring months is very pleasant. You can get some rainfall in the winter months, and the area is probably best avoided any later than February as from March onwards sand storms can get whipped up by the Shamal winds.

Philippines

Getting married in the Philippines is not without its complications but is possible for foreigners in certain circumstances and given the delightful – well, relatively delightful – climatic conditions in our autumn, winter and spring months, represents a lovely place to consider, especially when one or the other of the bridal couple are Filipino. Certainly the winter months from December to February create a drier climate and the months of November to February are generally cooler than during the rest of the year.

United Arab Emirates (UAE)

Abu Dhabi can be unbearably hot during our summer months but in the autumn, winter and spring daytime temperatures tend to be in the relatively comfortable high 20s to low 30s. You might even need to wear a jacket outdoors in the coolest winter months. In *Dubai*, the climate is similar. Unlike many of its neighbours, the UAE actively encourages tourism and Dubai, in particular, is becoming a very popular wedding venue. The ultra modern surroundings and first class hotels, airports, shops etc. are very appealing, as is the duty-free shopping in Dubai. And if you want to be reminded of the UAE's Bedouin roots, there are plenty of excursions and sights to see that celebrate this romantic culture.

Being a Muslim country the UAE's rules about alcohol are pretty strict, although it is available in hotels – at a price. Some say it's best to avoid travelling to the UAE during the period of Ramadan, as the services you need for your wedding celebrations may not be available.

As autumn, winter and spring are the peak tourist times in UAE, these are likely to be the most expensive months for a wedding celebration. I'm told that some of the hotels will give huge discounts if you plan your wedding in UAE during our summer months. But as the outdoor temperature is likely to be as much as 45°C and even the temperature of the ocean as much as 40°C (apparently outdoor swimming pools there have to be cooled, not heated) your wedding festivities would all have to be conducted indoors in the air conditioning.

Resources

I would like to express my grateful thanks to the wedding planners who have contributed to my research for this book. Some of their quotes appear in the book and I'm only sorry there wasn't room to include everyone's comments.

Needless to say they would be delighted to hear from you if you should decide to get professional help with your cooler-months wedding and judging by the quality of the information they all provided me with, they really do know their stuff.

They are (in alphabetical order according to first names):

Amanda Hibberd
Simply Scottish Weddings & Events
www.simply-scottish.com

Amanda Wright
Venus Wedding Plans
www.venusweddingplans.co.uk
www.belmontbridal.co.uk

Andrea Smith
Fabulous Day
www.fabulousday.co.uk

Bernadette Chapman
Dream Occasions
www.dream-occasions.co.uk

Beth Stretton
Get Married In France
www.getmarriedinfrance.co.uk

Beverley Morris Kafetzi
Unique Weddings Rhodes
www.uniqueweddingsrhodes.co.uk

Beverley Nichols
Jades Flower Design
http://www.jadesflowers.co.uk

Bridget Stott
Piece of Cake Party Planners
www.pieceofcakeuk.com

Carolyn Acton
Carolyn Acton Events
www.carolynactonevents.co.uk

Celine Prenassi
Piece Montee
www.piecemontee.com

Chris and Sue Odell
Artography Weddings
www.artography-weddings.co.uk

Claire
Wedding Services Spain
www.weddingservicespain.com

Claire Dobinson
Kiss The Frog
www.kissthefrog.biz

Danielle Watson
Astara Weddings & Events
www.astaraweddings.co.uk

Dawn Rennie
The Big Day Company
www.thebigdayco.biz

Debbie
Wedding Wonders
www.wedding-wonders.com

Deborah Taliani
Just get Married! Wedding Planners
www.justgetmarried.com

Emma Glen
Behind The Veil
www.behindtheveil.co.uk

Emma Jackson
Cherished Events
www.cherishedevents.co.uk

Emma Marygold
Marygold Weddings
www.marygoldweddings.com

Fanny Lesage
Histoires d'Envies
www.histoiresdenvies.com

Fiona Allen
Best Ideas International Wedding Planners
www.bestideasuk.com

Geraldine Borges
D'elite Spain Wedding Group
www.spain-wedding.com

Gianna Soria
Spain Wedding
www.spain-wedding.com

Gillian Gray
Jellybean Events Ltd
www.jellybeanevents.uk.com

Helen Bush and Lorraine Watson
Weddings by II Cool
www.weddingsbyiicool.com

James Lord
Love&Lord
www.loveandlord.com

Janet Sayer
Elizabeth Sayer Wedding Design Ltd
www.elizabethsayerweddings.co.uk

Janis MacLean
Highland Country Weddings Ltd
www.highlandcountryweddings.co.uk

Jeanette Obytz
Med Weddings
www.medweddings.com

Jenny Barnes
Make Our Day Events
www.makeourday.co.uk

Julie Tooby
Essentially You
http://www.essentially-you.net

Resources

Karen Brooks
A Perfect Plan
www.aperfectplan.co.uk

Kelly Chandler
The Bespoke Wedding Company
UK Alliance of Wedding Planners
www.thebespokeweddingco.com
www.ukawp.com

Laura and Victoria
www.lauraandvictoria.co.uk

Lauren
The Wedding Connection
www.theweddingconnection.info

Lisa Bevan
White Tulips Ltd Wedding Design & Coordination
www.weddingsbywhitetulips.com

Liz
Perfect Weddings and Parties
www.perfectweddingsandparties.co.uk

Liz Drake
Weddings Abroad by Spencer Scott
www.spencerscott.co.uk/weddings

Lucy Doherty
Weddings By Lucia
www.weddingsbylucia.com

Miguel Drudis
Golden Star Events
www.golden-star-events.com

Nick Cropper
Weddings & Honeymoons Abroad
www.weddings-abroad.com

Nikki
The Dream Wedding Company
www.thedreamweddingcompany.com

Odile Le Bris
Shalamar Flowers
www.shalamar-flowers.biz

Patricia Mallia
Mediterranean Weddings
www.wedinthemed.com

Sam
PT Weddings
www.ptweddings.com

Samantha Salisbury
Samantha Salisbury Weddings
www.samanthasalisburyweddings.co.uk

Sarah
Distinction Wedding Planners
www.distinctionweddings.co.uk

Sarah and Lesley
I Do Wedding Services
www.idoweddingservices.co.uk

Sarah Ducker
SJD Events
www.sjdevents.com

Resources

Sarah Williams
Heart To Heart
www.hearttoheartuk.co.uk

Sheila Chadha
The Indian Wedding Company
www.theindianweddingcompany.co.uk

Simone Butterfield
Dimples Events
www.dimplesevents.co.uk

Siobhan Craven-Robins
From This Day Forward
www.fromthisdayforward.co.uk

Sonia Abrams
Sparkle And Wow
www.sparkleandwow.co.uk

Sonita Gale
Time For You
www.time4you.co.uk

Steph
Marry Abroad
www.marryabroad.co.uk

Sue White
The White Wedding Company
www.whiteweddingcompany.com

Tammy Willson
Magic Dust – For Weddings
www.magic-dust.co.uk

Tara Nix
TDN Events
www.tdnevents.com

Teresa Di Mauro-Hadley
Party Punch
www.partypunch.co.uk

Theresa Guthrie
AWOL in Granada
www.awolgranada.com

Val
As You Like It Weddings
www.asyoulikeitweddings.co.uk

Vivienne McBride
Dragonfly
www.dragonflyweddingservices.co.uk

Zoë Lingard
Weddings by Zoë Lingard
www.zoelingard.co.uk

Websites

In my earlier weddings books you'll see that I have provided long lists of relevant websites but as time progresses and the internet gets ever larger and larger, to carry on doing that would be pointless, for two reasons. One, the lists would take up the whole book, and two, by the time you read this the websites and/or their URLs could well have changed.

This time, therefore, at the risk of being repetitious, in each instance where you may want to look for further information I have suggested the best search term or terms which you can put into 'your favourite search engine'. (Please note that to be politically correct I deliberately have avoided the G-word!) This should give you the happy result of the most up-to-date information available on the topic concerned.

Other books on winter weddings

At the time of writing (mid-2008), when you key '**winter weddings**' into the UK Amazon website, this book comes up as the first choice as it's already on preview. Other 'winter wedding', titles so far seem to be connected with fiction.

That does not mean to say that there won't be other books available in the future about weddings in the cooler months, so if you feel you want more information than that which I've provided here, you know what to do ... see above!

Other weddings books by How To Books

- How to Get Married in Green
- The A to Z of Wedding Worries and how to put them right
- Wedding speeches for Women
- Be the Best, Best Man and Make a Stunning Speech!
- The Complete Best Man
- Making the Best Man's Speech
- Making the Father of the Bride's Speech
- Raise your Glasses Please!

Index

Planning A Wedding Reception at Home

Carol Godsmark

This book will enable you to plan a wedding reception at home either with or without a caterer. There's a lot to think about: hiring the marquee, making sure you have everything that you need on hand — the things you take for granted if the reception is at a hotel, such as loos, adequate electrical power, parking, a stage for the band and lots more. This book will make sure you cover everything you need so the day goes smoothly

ISBN 978-1-84528-295-0

The Complete Father of the Bride

John Bowden

This book is packed with valuable tips and advice about conveying just the right messages to your daughter and her husband-to-be; understanding what is traditionally expected of you; establishing a good relationship with your future in-laws; getting best value for your hard-earned cash; giving sound financial and other guidance to the happy couple; keeping everyone calm and defusing any pre-wedding tension and conflicts; making a memorable speech — and ensuring everyone has a great time!

ISBN 978-1-84528-282-0

How To Get Married In Green

Suzan St Maur

'This thoroughly researched book is full of suggestions presented without preaching.' Wedding Cakes

'A fabulous, comprehensive guide for any bride (and groom) who are interested in planning a green wedding. Suzan gives great ideas, resources and advice from every step of eco-friendly wedding planning and she delivers it with charm and wit. Great ideas and a wealth of green information in a new and upbeat way.' www.feelgoodstyle.com

ISBN 978-1-84528-270-7

Wedding Planner

Elizabeth Catherine Myers

'Full of essential information, tips and ideas, and the handy task list will help make sure the preparation goes without a hitch.' Wedding Cakes

ISBN 978-1-84528-253-6

Making a Wedding Speech

John Bowden

'Do read Making a Wedding Speech.' — Virginia Ironside, The Sunday Mirror

'Packed with opening lines, jokes and model speeches. Invest in a copy.' — Brides Magazine

'A bible for nervous best men.' — Western Gazette

ISBN 978-1-84528-294-3

Be the Best, Best Man & Make a Stunning Speech

Phillip Khan-Panni

'Essential reading, and a great gift for those preparing to stand and deliver on the big day.' — Wedding Day

'Gives you all the low down on how to go about delivering a speech that will hold and impress the audience...also contains all the etiquette and do's and don'ts for the wedding as well as tips on helping to calm nerves.' — For the Bride

ISBN 978-1-85703-802-6

Making the Best Man's Speech

John Bowden

'If you want to project yourself as confident, clear, interesting, humorous and sensitive to the true meaning of the day whilst entertaining the assembled guests, buy it. My speech went down a storm, because it was written from the heart following the simple guidelines within this excellent and very accessible book.' Reader review

ISBN 978-1-85703-659-6

Making the Bridegroom's Speech

John Bowden

'Most of the advice I've seen on websites has either been painfully obvious or quite irrelevant to my situation. After a couple of hours reading this entertaining and helpful book, I was ready to start putting my speech together with confidence and optimism that I didn't have before. It's particularly helpful if you're concerned about how to convey sincere (and expected) emotions without your mates laughing at you!

It won't give you masses of content to crib from, though, but it does give enough guidance for you to produce your own material, which is probably better. Well worth the money.' Reader review

ISBN 978-1-85703-567-4

Making the Father of the Bride's Speech

John Bowden

If your daughter is getting married you will probably have to make a speech. You'll need this book. It contains all there is to know to give a speech that is both meaningful and joyous. This handy book will help to make your daughter's special day extra-special.

ISBN 978-1-85703-568-1

The Complete Best Man

John Bowden

'A valuable asset for the friend who didn't realise quite how much is involved in being his mate's best man!' – Wedding Dresses

'A lifesaver for a terrified best man.' – Pure Weddings

ISBN 978-1-84528-104-5

The A to Z of Wedding Worries

... and how to put them right

Suzan St Maur

'The must-read book for brides-to-be.' Ulster Bride

'Many useful topics all covered with a good dose of humour, essential if you are to keep sane whilst organising a/your wedding!' Cake Craft & Decoration

'Covers all aspects of getting married from animals at weddings to who pays for what, laid out in an easy-to-read format.' Wedding Venues and Services

ISBN 978-184528-172-4

Wedding Speeches For Women

Suzan St Maur

'It's no longer just the men who get to speak at weddings — here's help for female speakers to plan their timing and content including jokes, poems and quotations.' — Pure Weddings

'The perfect gift for those special people who have agreed to be part of your special day.' Wedding Dresses

ISBN 978-1-84528-107-6

Get Wed for Less — A Bride's Guide

Liz Bright

'A must have for any bride to be! The book really does cover every aspect of wedding planning and gives great money saving tips. It was incredibly helpful and took the stress out of planning the wedding. I found the check lists especially useful and the day went without a hitch! Thank you.' Amazon Reader

ISBN 978-1-84528-210-3